Res Judicata and Collateral Estoppel

Recent Titles from Quorum Books

Current Budgeting Practices in U.S. Industry: The State of the Art
Srinivasan Umapathy

Developing Negotiation Skills in Sales Personnel: A Guide to Price Realization for Sales Managers and Sales Trainers
David A. Stumm

Training in the Automated Office: A Decision-Maker's Guide to Systems Planning and Implementation
Randy J. Goldfield

The Strategist CEO: How Visionary Executives Build Organizations
Michel Robert

America's Future in Toxic Waste Management: Lessons from Europe
Bruce W. Piasecki and Gary A. Davis

Telecommunications Management for the Data Processing Executive: A Decision-Maker's Guide to Systems Planning and Implementation
Milburn D. Smith III

The Political Economy of International Debt: What, Who, How Much, and Why?
Michel Henri Bouchet

Multinational Risk Assessment and Management: Strategies for Investment and Marketing Decisions
Wenlee Ting

Supply-Side Portfolio Strategies
Victor A. Canto and Arthur B. Laffer, editors

Staffing the Contemporary Organization: A Guide to Planning, Recruiting, and Selecting for Human Resource Professionals
Donald L. Caruth, Robert M. Noe III, and R. Wayne Mondy

The Court and Free-Lance Reporter Profession: Improved Management Strategies
David J. Saari

Pollution Law Handbook: A Guide to Federal Environmental Laws
Sidney M. Wolf

RES JUDICATA AND COLLATERAL ESTOPPEL

Tools for Plaintiffs and Defendants

Warren Freedman

Q
Quorum Books
NEW YORK · WESTPORT, CONNECTICUT · LONDON

Library of Congress Cataloging-in-Publication Data

Freedman, Warren.
Res Judicata and Collateral Estoppel.
Bibliography: p.
Includes index.
1. Res judicata—United States. 2. Estoppel—
United States. I. Title.
KF8992.F74 1988 347.73′504 87-7307
347.307504
ISBN 0-89930-277-7 (lib. bdg. : alk. paper)

British Library Cataloguing in Publication Data is available.

Library of Congress Catalog Card Number: 87-7307
ISBN: 0-89930-277-7

First published in 1988 by Quorum Books

Greenwood Press, Inc.
88 Post Road West, Westport, Connecticut 06881

Printed in the United States of America

The paper used in this book complies with the Permanent Paper Standard issued by the National Information Standards Organization (Z39.48-1984).

10 9 8 7 6 5 4 3 2 1

Contents

Res Judicata and Collateral Estoppel

1

Definitions and Terminology

Thirty years ago a professor wrote that ''salutary as the basic principle of Res Judicata undoubtedly is, one of its aspects in particular, the doctrine of Collateral Estoppel, is an extraordinarily dangerous instrument. Over and over again it has been demonstrated that, in the use of this doctrine, courts must be alert to the danger that its extension by merely logical processes of manipulation may produce results which are abhorrent to the sense of justice and to orderly law administration.''[1]

Collateral estoppel is but one of the three constituents of the principle of res judicata, the other two being merger (which occurs when a money judgment for the plaintiff, for example, merges his cause of action, terminating the original cause of action on the judgment) and bar (which means that a judgment on the merits has been rendered for the defendant, for example, and the original cause of action has been terminated).[2] Basically, res judicata is that principle inherent in all judicial systems which provides that ''an existing final judgment rendered upon the merits, without fraud or collusion, by a court of competent jurisdiction, is conclusive of rights, questions, and facts in issue, as to the parties and their privies, in all other actions in the same or any other judicial tribunal of concurrent jurisdiction.''[3] Res judicata is a common law doctrine that signifies ''claim or cause of action preclusion'' in contrast to collateral estoppel, which is ''issue or fact preclusion.'' But the broad range of res judicata encompasses an entire class of concepts such as election of remedies, splitting of action, full faith and credit, and comity.[4] Estoppel, as well as these important concepts, has the same general objective as res judicata, to wit: finality of litigation. In federal practice, for example, there is a statutory provision for the application of res judicata and collateral estoppel, 28 USC 1738, which requires that all legislative acts of a state and records and judicial proceedings of any state court which are authenticated pursuant to statutes "shall have same full faith and credit in every court within the United States and its Territories or Possessions as they have by law or usage in the courts of such state, Territory or Possession from which they are taken."[5]

Collateral estoppel, derived from the French word *estoupe*, was applied originally to prevent a party from challenging the validity of a legal record including his own deed, but the English courts of equity developed the doctrine later as a general principle of preventing a party from taking an inequitable advantage of a predicament in which his own conduct had placed his adversary. The doctrine was then taken over by English common law judges as a device to enable them to lengthen their judicial arm and afford relief which courts of equity had always offered.[6] A warehouseman who represented that he holds goods for another in response to an inquiry by an intending purchaser from the bailor,[7] or one who informs such a purchaser that his signature forged to a negotiable instrument is genuine,[8] may be estopped to deny the truth of the statement if the purchase is made in reliance upon his statement or conduct, for example. This equitable estoppel may be based upon some definite misrepresentation of fact, made with reason to believe that another will rely upon it, and the other person does rely in changing his position to his advantage.[9] Equitable estoppel may also be based on a mere failure to take action, as where a party stands by and allows another to deal with his property or to incur some liability toward him without informing the other of his mistake, for example.[10] But equitable estoppel must be distinguished from collateral estoppel, which is designed not necessarily to do justice under the particular circumstances of the case but to preclude the relitigation of the facts and/or issues of the case.

Collateral estoppel is delineated in Section 17 and 20 of Restatement (Second) of Judgments as purely a "preclusion" concept: "When an issue of fact or law is actually litigated and determined by a valid and final judgment, and the determination is essential to the judgment, the determination is conclusive in a subsequent action between the parties, whether on the same or a different claim." Collateral estoppel is applicable only when the issue or the fact to be precluded in the subsequent suit was essentially identical to the issue or the fact decided in the original suit,[11] was actually adjudicated[12] by a final and valid judgment,[13] and the issue or the fact was essential to reaching the original judgment.[14] The U.S. Supreme Court in Kremer v. Chemical Construction Corp.[15] in 1982 observed that the party to the original action must also have had a "full and fair opportunity to litigate" the issue or the fact, a declaration by the highest court that the equitable and discretionary nature of collateral estoppel is well recognized.[16] Three years earlier in Montana v. United States[17] the same court held that collateral estoppel was applicable only when no "special circumstances" (here the adequacy of state trial procedure) warranted an exception to the normal rules of preclusion. Equitable principles must be given due consideration, as illustrated by Donovan v. Cunningham,[18] where the Fifth U.S.

Court of Appeals ruled that the government was not estopped from relitigating the claim because the prior suit did not vindicate broader governmental interests.

On the other hand, in Niagara Frontier Tariff Bureau, Inc. v. United States (——F2d——[2nd Cir., Aug. 20, 1987]), a petitioner who sought judicial review of an order of the Interstate Commerce Commission was "collaterally estopped from relitigating its challenge to the Commission's interpretation of the statute." The Second U.S. Court of Appeals found that the case presented "identical issues and identical parties, and petitioner alleges neither changes in controlling facts or law, nor any special circumstances to warrant an exception to the principles of collateral estoppel." The court concluded that relitigation was barred because "resolution of this issue was 'necessary and essential to the judgment in (the earlier action).' " (Citing Wickham Contracting Co. v. Board of Education, 715 F2d 21 [2nd Cir., 1983].)

In Sucher v. Kutscher's Country Club[19] plaintiffs sued the hotel in 1980 after the female plaintiff fell from her wheelchair while using a chairlifting machine at the hotel in 1979. Alleging a defect in the machine, the defendant hotel impleaded the vendor and installer of the chairlifting machine; these new defendants then impleaded in 1982 the manufacturer of the machine. In 1984 the third and fourth defendants successfully moved for summary judgment, and the court dismissed the third and fourth party complaints on the basis that the hotel's pleadings offered evidence of only negligence in the installation of the machine. In mid-1984 the hotel served a new third party complaint against the machine manufacturer, and the machine manufacturer moved to dismiss on the ground of collateral estoppel. While the New York trial court accepted this defense, the New York Appellate Division, Second Dept., deemed the dismissal

> an improvident exercise of discretion: The doctrine of collateral estoppel applies to preclude relitigation of an issue where it is found that (1) the issue sought to be precluded is identical to one which was necessarily decided in a prior proceeding, and (2) the litigant against whom preclusion is sought in the present proceeding had a full and fair opportunity to litigate the issue in the prior proceeding. . . . The burden of establishing the first element is upon the proponent of preclusion, and the burden of establishing the second is upon the opponent. . . . At bar, respondent clearly met its burden of showing that the identical issue of the existence of a defect, and more specifically, of any defect relating to the machine's inability to provide a passenger with a smooth transition from loading ramp to floor, was necessarily determined adversely to Kutscher's when Judge Christ granted summary judgment. Kutscher's arguments to the contrary ignore the allegations in the pleadings. However, identity of a necessarily determined issue is only the first part of Collateral Estoppel analysis.

The court continued:

> The second part is an inquiry as to whether the party sought to be precluded had a full and fair opportunity to litigate that issue in the prior proceeding. Many factors have

been identified as bearing upon the full and fair opportunity analysis, including the availability of new evidence, the use of initiative, the extent of the prior litigation, and the competence and experience of counsel. . . . At bar, Kutscher's presented new evidence, a design evaluation report, as part of its opposition to the instant motion to dismiss. This report was not prepared until more than three months after the summary judgment motion was decided by Justice Christ, and contains material which would unquestionably have produced a different result by raising substantial fact issues regarding the existence of design defects.

The New York appellate court concluded:

Collateral Estoppel or issue preclusion is founded upon policy considerations and judicial recognition of aims which seek, inter alia, to conserve the resources of the courts and litigants. . . . Applicability of the doctrine must be determined on a case-by-case basis, without rigidity . . . and the overall fairness of applying the doctrine must be the crowning consideration.[20]

On the other hand, the New York Court of Appeals in Kaufman v. Eli Lilly & Co.[21] in 1985 ruled that the defendant product manufacturer was precluded from relitigating five of the six issues decided by the jury; only the issue of "concerted action," which alleged that defendant had acted in concert with other drug product manufacturers in testing and marketing the product for use in treating pregnancy accidents, was given "collateral estoppel effect."[22] In Welch v. Philip Morris, Inc.[23] the plaintiff, an actor who had performed in a 1967 cigarette commercial on TV, sued for equitable relief and damages under Section 51 of the New York Civil Rights Law, charging invasion of his privacy, when the defendant broadcasting company reran the commercial as part of a retrospective on great television commercials. In a federal court suit the defendants won a directed verdict at trial. Then the same defendants moved for summary judgment on collateral estoppel grounds, and the New York Supreme Court, New York County, agreed, finding that

the pleadings in the state court action raise issues which are virtually identical to those considered in the federal action. The doctrine of Collateral Estoppel was developed to prevent a party in one action from relitigating issues already decided against him in another action. . . . Here the gravamen of each complaint is the claim of an unauthorized use of plaintiff's picture and portrait for advertising or purposes of trade. The court in the federal action directed a verdict in favor of [defendants] after finding that plaintiff, after presenting all his evidence, had failed to prove a prima facie case under Section 51 of the Civil Rights Law. The court found plaintiff's consent led to the use of his portrait or picture. . . . plaintiff's attempt to distinguish the issues in these two actions by referring to the federal ban on cigarette advertising . . . [is] unpersuasive.

It should be observed that res judicata, or "claim or cause of action preclusion," is non-discretionary in nature because without res judicata the judgment lacks conclusiveness and essential finality.[24] On the other hand, the application of collateral estoppel is discretionary in nature because it primarily serves to promote judicial economy, an important but not a necessary commodity.[25] Non-discretionary application of res judicata is complex and often unpredictable: for example, some courts consider the "second case" as involving the same cause of action or the same claim when it relates to the same subject matter,[26] the same legal issues,[27] or the same essential facts[28] involved in the first case; while other courts predicate application of res judicata on the impairment of legal rights created in the first case.[29] In effect, the doctrine of res judicata bars not only relitigation of claims and causes of action that were actually decided in the first case, but also those claims and causes of action that could have been raised and decided in the first case.[30] Collateral estoppel, or "issue or fact preclusion," is similarly subject to different interpretations from jurisdiction to jurisdiction.[31] Generally, collateral estoppel operates to bar relitigation of an issue or fact by the parties to the prior action where a court of competent jurisdiction has previously decided the issue in a final adjudication on the merits.[32] Some courts apply collateral estoppel only where the resolution of the issue or fact in question was essential or necessary to support the prior judgment.[33]

It is interesting to observe that federal courts have shown reluctance to apply either res judicata or collateral estoppel to prior state determinations in civil rights litigation. The point is simply that these doctrines of finality would here preclude a party from seeking federal remedies after state proceedings or state administrative rulings; and therefore these doctrines, if applied, might defeat congressional policy of giving highest priority to national civil rights violations and achieving some uniformity throughout the United States.[34]

2

Historical Perspectives

Res judicata is a product of Roman law which simply stated that an earlier adjudication was conclusive in a second suit involving the same principal issues and same legal bases.[35] In Roman law res judicata rested upon the sanctity of the final judicial pronouncement. It was not until the twelfth century that the res judicata doctrine became part of English law.[36]

The origins of collateral estoppel were apparently Germanic, and were based on the premise that the parties having dominated the judicial proceedings, their acts created a true estoppel against future relitigation.[37] Gradually this concept was transformed into a form of estoppel by record, as expressed in 1831 in the English decision of King v. Carlisle:[38] the record was indeed then the best evidence of determinations in the prior proceeding that bound the parties. It was the prior determination, not the final judgment, that was the source of collateral estoppel. Finality of judgment ''belonged'' to res judicata, while equitable considerations governed collateral estoppel: it was unfair for a party to claim subsequently a different conduct or different position, i.e., equitable estoppel, although early English decisions also predicated collateral estoppel upon a final judgment so as to be certain that the process of issue or fact resolution had concluded.[39]

The U.S. Supreme Court in 1877 in Cromwell v. County of Sac[40] had occasion to articulate the historical distinctions in a case involving plaintiff's efforts to recover on bonds and interest coupons allegedly issued by the defendant. The defense was based upon the 1870 decision of Smith v. Sac County,[41] which denied recovery to that plaintiff in an action to collect on earlier maturing coupons of the same bonds. The defendant County in the earlier case argued that the bonds were not validly authorized or issued; the U.S. Supreme

Court then ruled in 1870 that "the said bonds and coupons were wholly void as against said County," and that there was evidence that the bonds had been fraudulently issued and that the plaintiff Smith was not a holder for value entitled to collect. The highest court in 1877 ruled that when the same claim is involved in two separate actions between the same parties a judgment on the merits against the plaintiff in the first case absolutely bars prosecution of the second case. Every matter which was presented or which might have been presented was barred in the second case. But when the second case is on a different claim, the prior judgment will estop only those matters "in issue or points controverted, upon the determination of which the finding or verdict was rendered."[42] Thus, the earlier case was a complete bar to further litigation regarding the coupons, but the bonds and coupons in the later Cromwell case[43] were not among the bonds and coupons in the Smith case,[44] and therefore res judicata was inapplicable to the second case. The issue of the legality of the bonds, however, was precluded under the doctrine of collateral estoppel.[45]

It was not until 1942 that the landmark California decision of Bernhard v. Bank of America[46] removed the mutuality restriction from the doctrine of collateral estoppel, and expanded utilization of the doctrine of collateral estoppel became the order of the day. Justice Traynor's reformulation of collateral estoppel required affirmative answers to three question: "Was the issue decided in the prior adjudication identical with the one presented in the action in question? Was there a final judgment on the merits? Was the party against whom the plea is asserted a party or in privity with a party to the prior adjudication?"[47] Here there was an interbank transfer of funds from the decedent's Los Angeles bank to another account in another place, where it was withdrawn by the executor of her estate as a gift to himself; after the executor resigned, his accounting did not mention the "gift," but the probate court found that the transferred funds were indeed a "gift" made by the decedent during her lifetime. The new executor sued all the defendants to recover the "gift" for the estate, but the California Supreme Court found that the real parties in interest against whom collateral estoppel was invoked were the same beneficiaries of the estate. It is interesting to speculate as to the decision if the probate court here was an administrative agency and not a judicial body, for under Pearson v. Williams[48] the U.S. Supreme Court in 1906 had characterized an administrative agency barring aliens from entering the United States as an instrument of the executive branch of government not entitled to res judicata attention! In 1932 in Crowell v. Benson[49] the U.S. Supreme Court refused to give full res judicata effect to findings made by the U.S. Employers' Compensation Commission in deciding workers' compensation claims under the Longshoremen's and Harbor Workers' Compensation Act.[50] However, in 1940 in Sunshine Anthracite Coal Co. v. Adkins[51] the highest court faced a different situation and ruled that collateral estoppel should be applied: here the National Bituminous Coal Commission had found that the petitioner's coal was "bituminous" and therefore should not be exempt from a special sales tax. When the Internal

Revenue Service attempted to collect the special tax, petitioner sued in the federal court to enjoin the tax collection on the ground that the Bituminous Coal Act was unconstitutional and the petitioner was not subject to its provisions. The federal district court upheld the constitutionality of the Act and ruled that the petitioner was estopped from relitigating the status of its coal. The highest court affirmed, and agreed that collateral estoppel was applicable to the identical issue of the status of petitioner's coal. In 1966 in United States v. Utah Construction & Mining Co.[52] full acceptance for collateral estoppel to apply to administrative findings helped to reduce the judicial caseload.[53] Interestingly, Section 83 (1) of Restatement (Second) of Judgments endorsed res judicata and collateral estoppel as applicable to administrative determinations "except [where it would be incompatible with a legislative policy], a valid and final adjudicative determination by an administrative tribunal has the same effects under the rule of res judicata, subject to the same exceptions and qualifications, as a judgment of a court."

In 1979 in Parklane Hosiery Co. v. Shore[54] the U.S. Supreme Court allowed a summary proceeding to displace a judicial resolution of issues, and granted the trial court virtually unreviewable discretion to do likewise. Here corporate management allegedly violated federal securities laws by issuing a materially false and misleading proxy statement in connection with a merger. A stockholders' class action seeking damages, rescission of the merger, and costs was brought, and at the same time the Securities and Exchange Commission (SEC) moved to enjoin the tortfeasors. The SEC action resulted in judgment against the tortfeasors, and the stockholders sought to use the issues decided in the SEC case against Parklane in their class action suit. The highest court found for the stockholders by collaterally estopping Parklane from relitigating the issues resolved against them in the SEC action.[55] Thus, offensive use of collateral estoppel was approved, despite the fact that the SEC determination had found that Parklane's proxy statement was false in only one respect and that the major relief requested, i.e., an injunction against further violations of the federal securities laws and appointment of a special counsel to determine the fair market value of Parklane's shares for the sake of its public stockholders, was denied! It is submitted that the SEC findings were not essential to the judgment in the stockholders' class action, and therefore probably should not have been given collateral estoppel effect.[56]

The same year the highest court in Montana v. United States[57] applied collateral estoppel against the United States, based on a Montana Supreme Court case in which the United States controlled the litigation and had a financial interest in the outcome of the case. In 1980 in Allen v. McCurry[58] the same court held that the doctrines of res judicata and collateral estoppel are applicable to civil rights claims brought in the federal courts under 42 USC 1983.[59]

3

Essential Elements of Res Judicata: Preclusion by Prior Adjudication

Res judicata has today sloughed off many of the attributes of rigidity which were characteristic of its antecedents in Roman law.[60] Today res judicata may be said to be imbued with the administrative traditions of equity litigation, as it seeks not to fragmentize disputes but to bring together parties and claims in pragmatic fashion so as to do justice.[61] Indeed, res judicata has assumed many aspects of public law in the sense that this doctrine of preclusion by prior adjudication has less exclusively focused upon honoring *a priori* rights and has more concerned itself with balancing the need to achieve a fair and just result in individual cases. Res judicata expresses the public policy of economizing judicial resources as well as the resources of the parties. Its interest in finality of claims and of causes of action as well as issues and facts pertaining thereto is conducive to the greater public interest.[62] The U.S. Supreme Court in 1907 in Kessler v. Eldred[63] echoed this sentiment of finality:

> This judgment, whether it proceeds upon good reasons, whether it was right or wrong, settled finally and everywhere . . . that Kessler had the right to manufacture, use and sell the electric cigar lighter before the court. . . . If rights between litigants are once established by the final judgment of a court of competent jurisdiction, those rights must be recognized in every way . . . by those who are bound by it.[64]

Res judicata fosters respect for the determinations of the original tribunal, for it enhances the predictability and consistency of those determinations. The preclusive effect of res judicata extends not only to those defenses or grounds of recovery actually presented, but also to those defenses or grounds of recovery which could have been offered but were in fact not offered.[65] Furthermore, the actual parties to the suit, as well as those in privity with them, are barred from future litigation by the judgment.[66]

In 1813 in Ferrer's Case[67] Lord Coke stated the goals of res judicata to be the avoidance of

> infiniteness of verdicts, recoveries and judgments in one and the same case. . . . Sometimes contrarieties of verdicts and judgments one against the other . . . and the continuance of suits for 20, 30, and 40 years, to the utter impoverishing of the parties. . . . All this tends to the dishonor of the common law, which utterly abhors infiniteness and delaying of suits.

Professor Vestal centuries later [in 1969] observed these goals as (a) establishing and fixing the rights of individuals; (b) avoiding the harassment of the parties which usually results from repetitious litigation; (c) using the judicial system efficiently; and (d) preserving the prestige of the courts by avoiding inconsistent verdicts.[68] The U.S. Supreme Court in 1979 added the goals of (e) relief given the parties from the cost and vexation of multiple lawsuits; (f) the conservation of judicial resources; and (g) the prevention of inconsistent decisions to encourage reliance on judgments.[69]

The important distinction between res judicata and collateral estoppel is noted by the U.S. Supreme Court:

> Under the doctrine of Res Judicata, a judgment "on the merits" in a prior suit involving the same parties or their privies bars a second suit based on the same cause of action. Under the doctrine of Collateral Estoppel, on the other hand, such a judgment precludes relitigation of issues actually litigated and determined in the prior suit, regardless of whether it was based on the same cause of action as the second suit.[70]

Among the essential elements of res judicata are (1) identity of parties; (2) identity of claim or cause of action; (3) validity and finality of judgment, award, or order of the court or tribunal; (4) full opportunity to be heard; (5) damages and seriousness of the allegations; (6) inconsistent verdicts or judgments; and (7) full faith and credit, as delineated hereinafter in Chapter 3.

3.1 IDENTITY OF PARTIES AND RES JUDICATA

Identity of parties is an essential element of res judicata because only parties or their privies are bound by a prior adjudication of the claim or cause of action. This doctrine of "mutuality" means that the parties in the second suit must be the same or in privity with the parties in the first suit.[71] The requisite of privity rests on due process considerations, to wit: it is unconstitutional under the Fifth and Fourteenth amendments to the U.S. Constitution for a court to preclude a party from supporting or negating a claim or cause of action which was adjudicated in a prior trial in which that party had no notice and in which that party did not participate.[72] Indeed, the "party or privity" prerequisite is "undisputable as a matter of constitutional law."[73] The California decision of Meldrim v. Board of Supervisors[74] illustrates the point: here a prior judgment in a mandamus proceeding (which upheld an initiative ordinance fixing salaries of members of the board of supervisors) that had been brought against the county rather than against the supervisors as public officers was not res judicata as to the subsequent action brought against the board of supervisors itself attacking the particular salary increase as a violation of the initiative ordinance, because the identity of parties necessary for res judicata was not present. Similarly, the New Hampshire decision of Sanderson v. Greenland[75] holds that plaintiffs (whose subdivision building permits were denied) were not barred from litigating the validity of the zoning amendment that prohibited the subdivision, even though validity of the zoning amendment may have been an issue that went to judgment in litigation between the governmental entity and other parties, since neither res judicata nor collateral estoppel applies to persons who are not parties nor in privity with parties to previous litigation in which the issue was decided. It is the stranger in the midst that seeks to prevent or to sanction the relitigation of the claim or the cause of action that raises the important issue of "mutuality."

Mutuality usually centers about the concept of fairness in the sense that it is unfair to allow a person to reap the benefits of a favorable judgment or award to which he was not a party.[76] Other arguments in favor of mutuality include the likelihood of compromise verdicts,[77] the incompetence of the attorney in the previous action,[78] newly discovered evidence,[79] and the fallibility of the jury system.[80] In the Louisiana case of Caulfield v. Fidelity & Casualty Co.[81] the Fifth U.S. Court of Appeals simply stated that the Louisiana Civil Code required identity of parties, which was not present, and therefore res judicata was inapplicable. The U.S. Supreme Court in Lawlor v. National Screen Service[82] held that a judgment dismissing with prejudice a suit for treble damages under the antitrust laws did not bar a subsequent suit for such damages based on conduct subsequent to the earlier judgment with respect to these defendants, who were not parties to the former suit. The highest court disagreed with the lower federal court, which had held that the relationship of these defendants to the other defendants was "close enough to bring them all within the scope of the doctrine of Res Judicata." The highest court pointed out that those defendants were not parties to the earlier suit, nor did they come within the orthodox categories of privies, and furthermore could not have been joined in the earlier suit, nor was there any obligation to join them since as joint tortfeasors they were not indispensable parties. Section 93 of Restatement (Second) of Judgments approved the mutuality rule, referring to the following illustrations: "A and B collide, harming C. C brings an action against A on the ground that A was negligent. In this action it is found that C was guilty of contributory negligence and judgment is given for A. In a subsequent action by C against B, the question as to the contributory negligence of C is not Res Judicata."[83] And

"A and B are passengers in a car driven by C which collides with a car driven by D. A brings action against D and obtains judgment on the ground that D was negligent. This finding is not Res Judicata in a subsequent proceeding brought by B against D."[84]

But exceptions to the rule of mutuality became the order of the day, as illustrated by Section 99 of Restatement (Second) of Judgments:

> A valid judgment on the merits and not based on a personal defense, in favor of a person charged with the commission of a tort or a breach of contract, bars a subsequent action by the plaintiff against another responsible for the conduct of such person if the action is based solely upon the existence of a tort or breach of contract by such person, whether or not the other person has a right of indemnity.

In Thomas v. Consolidation Coal Co.[85] the Fourth U.S. Court of Appeals held that the union was bound by the former judgment because the plaintiffs-employees could prevail in the instant suit against the union only if they proved that the officials and representatives of the union who represented the plaintiffs in the grievance procedure acted fraudulently; and that in their suit against those officials and representatives of the union in the state court, plaintiffs had had their day in court and, being unsuccessful therein, it was not unfair that they should be denied a subsequent action against the union. The court concluded that the union was entitled to the benefit of the state court dismissal of the individual defendants. Indeed, "the rigid restriction of the rule of mutuality has been corroded by the expansion of the concept of privity and the creation of numerous exceptions to the rule."[86]

It was not until 1942 in Bernhard v. Bank of America[87] that the requirement of mutuality was abandoned by the California Supreme Court, although the case involved the defensive use of collateral estoppel.[88] Justice Traynor, writing for a unanimous court, analyzed the rule of mutuality and found no basis in reason for prohibiting a non-party from estopping a plaintiff who had lost the same issue in a prior suit. The U.S. Supreme Court in 1971 placed its imprimatur on the concept of nonmutuality when it ruled in Blonder-Tongue Laboratories, Inc. v. University of Illinois Foundation[89] that the defensive use of collateral estoppel was permissible in the patent case before the court: "The uncritical acceptance of the principle of mutuality . . . is today out of place. . . . Whether it is any longer tenable to afford a litigant more than one full and fair opportunity for judicial resolution of the same issue" is indeed questionable.

The abandonment of the mutuality rule does not mean that now a stranger to a judgment has an absolute right to rely, irrespective of the circumstances, upon the res judicata effect of a judgment to which his adversary was a party.[90] As the federal court in Nevada in United States v. United Airlines, Inc.[91] observed: "[T]he rule of non-mutuality is not a general one but a limited one to be determined from the facts and circumstances in each case whether or not it should be applied." The New York Court of Appeals in Schwartz v. Public

Administrator[92] in 1969 ruled that New York had replaced the rule of mutuality with the adoption of a full and fair opportunity test, discussed herein at Section 3.4.

3.2 IDENTICAL CLAIM OR CAUSE OF ACTION

Another essential element of res judicata is the identity of the claim or the cause of action, i.e., the parties are precluded by the prior adjudication if the claim or cause of action was identical with the claim or cause of action in the first action. Section 24 of Restatement (Second) of Judgments defines "claim" as including all rights to remedies with respect to a "transaction, or series of connected transactions." The federal district court in Pennsylvania in County of Lancaster v. Philadelphia Electric Co.[93] ruled that a civil rights damages action by the county and school district against the state and state supreme court for alleged denial of the right to tax certain property was barred by res judicata where the same claim was previously litigated in an action by the same plaintiffs against other defendants in state courts.

The identical "cause of action" as the basis for preclusion under res judicata entails some difficulty, for the courts that harp upon the fact that under common law and code pleading

> the smallest unit cognizable by courts is the cause of action, which, because it is directly descended from the forms of action, is a rigid and precisely defined plea. Often, it is not broad enough to encompass all the factual and legal justifications which might be used in resolving the underlying factual dispute. In other circumstances, several causes of action might be available for a party to seek redress in a particular factual dispute.[94]

In Leonard v. Schall[95] the Minnesota court held that a prior unsuccessful suit on a contract did not bar a second suit on quantum meruit. Indeed, the U.S. Supreme Court in 1876 had ruled that res judicata, or claim preclusion, would not prevent relitigation because only the very cause of action previously asserted was barred.[96] Today, since the litigation unit is the much broader "claim," it is difficult for a litigant to propound a theory of recovery that could not have been asserted in the first case; consequently, res judicata is the primary mechanism for preventing relitigation of the same issues between the same parties.[97]

In distinguishing res judicata from collateral estoppel it is important to note that the doctrine of res judicata does not preclude any single issue, as does collateral estoppel. Res judicata acts as a bar to further litigation of the cause of action between the same parties as to every issue or set of facts or defense raised and also as to those which may have been presented. This application of res judicata is known as preventing "the splitting of a cause of action."[98] In Dill v. Avery[99] the plaintiff sued the defendant for personal injuries arising from an automobile accident; later plaintiff sued for property damages, and defendant argued that res judicata barred the subsequent claim for property damages. The Maryland court agreed that the property damages claim was barred under the Maryland Code, which does not authorize the splitting of property damage claims from other claims arising out of automobile accidents. The court held that a claim for property damages and a claim for personal injuries arising from a single wrongful or negligent act constituted a single cause of action.

3.3 VALIDITY AND FINALITY OF JUDGMENT OR AWARD

Another essential element of res judicata is the validity and finality of the judgment or award. The underlying policy here is to minimize the judicial energy devoted to individual cases, to establish certainty and respect for court judgment or tribunal award, and to protect the party relying on the prior adjudication from vexatious litigation. In the New York case of Schuylkill Fuel Corp. v. Nieberg Realty Corp.[100] the New York Court of Appeals in 1929 defined "finality" in terms of whether the rights and interests which were established by the first judgment or award would be destroyed or impaired by litigation of the second action. The U.S. Supreme Court in 1876 opined that

> the judgment, if rendered upon the merits, constitutes an absolute bar to a subsequent action. It is a finality as to the claim or demand in controversy, concluding parties and those in privity with them, not only as to every matter which was offered and received to sustain or defeat the claim or demand, but as to any other admissible matter which might have been offered for that purpose. . . . Such demand or claim, having passed into judgment, cannot again be brought into litigation between the parties in proceedings at law upon any ground whatever.[101]

Professors Callen and Kadue in 1980 observed that

> finality allows the parties to plan their conduct outside the judicial forum, whether by allowing them to use resources for purposes other than judicial battle, by encouraging them to behave in ways approved by the prior decision, by discouraging them from behaving in a manner they know to be illegal, or by preventing the estopped party from using the threat of relitigation to extract concessions from a person who was not a person to the prior action.[102]

In bankruptcy practice the issue of finality is important, as illustrated by the U.S. Supreme Court decision in Brown v. Felsen.[103] Here the highest court considered whether a prior state court judgment which did not include a finding of fraud was res judicata in subsequent dischargeability litigation; if the doctrine of res judicata applied, the creditor would be unable to introduce, in the dischargeability action, evidence of fraud, and the debt would be discharged. The Court held that the prior state court judgment based on an action in which the fraud issue had not been litigated was not res judicata or binding on the Bankruptcy Court in the dischargeability litigation. To give res judicata effect to the state court judgment would defeat congressional policy embodied in the

1970 amendments to the Bankruptcy Code. Indeed, the parties had had little incentive to litigate fully the dischargeability issue, and the Court refused to decide whether collateral estoppel might be applicable, because that issue had not been presented to the Court. While the Brown v. Felsen case resolved the res judicata question with respect to pre-bankruptcy judgments, the highest court did not address the question of post-bankruptcy judgments, although the Bankruptcy Court for the Southern District of New York did so in In Re Aurre, Jr.[104] Here a wife who claimed she was owed money under a pre-bankruptcy separation agreement brought an action on the agreement in state court after her debtor-husband received his discharge in bankruptcy. Under Section 523 (a)(5) of the Bankruptcy Code the husband's obligation would be discharged if the agreement involved property but not if it concerned alimony, maintenance, or child support. The wife obtained a default judgment, and when she tried to enforce her default judgment, the husband obtained an order reopening the bankruptcy and sought to have the separation agreement declared to involve property settlement, which meant that his obligation was discharged under bankruptcy. But the court refused to disturb the default judgment which the Bankruptcy Court construed as res judicata, giving finality to the determination of the state court on the post-bankruptcy separation agreement. But it should be pointed out that the res judicata issue can arise only when the state court has concurrent jurisdiction with the Bankruptcy Court and when the dischargeability issue was or could have been raised in the state court proceeding after the bankruptcy.

3.4 FULL AND FAIR OPPORTUNITY TO BE HEARD

In Parklane Hosiery Co. v. Shore[105] the U.S. Supreme Court in 1979 emphasized the need for a full opportunity to be heard before imposing any preclusion upon the parties. For example, a defendant may face massive damages in subsequent suits by unforeseeable plaintiffs after he loses the issue of liability in the first suit.[106] A defendant may be sued repeatedly by multiple plaintiffs who stay out of the original suit although joinder is possible. Multiple suits by successive plaintiffs may expose a defendant to inconsistent verdicts, inter alia.[107] Thus, it is self-evident that a full opportunity to be heard is an essential element of res judicata, i.e., the risk of unfairness must be overcome if claim preclusion or cause of action preclusion is to be allowed. Where the opportunity to litigate was not complete and unfettered,[108] the court should not grant preclusion because fundamental unfairness is existent.

Among the many factors bearing upon this issue of unfairness or lack of full opportunity to be heard are the inconvenience of the forum where plaintiff has brought suit, the likelihood of a compromise verdict, a verdict for the plaintiff that represented a compromise between damages and liability, and the lack of incentive.[109] This lack of incentive to litigate is intangible; it means that, although a defendant received every procedural opportunity, he simply was not motivated under the circumstances to present a full and complete defense.[110] When the liability is limited or small, the defense tends to be less vigorous, and giving effect subsequently to the weak effort at defense appears to be unfair. In Berner v. British Commonwealth Pacific Airlines, Ltd.[111] the Second U.S. Circuit Court of Appeals implied that "incentive" was distinct from the procedural opportunity to be heard: "While not necessarily suggesting that defendant did not have a 'full and fair opportunity to litigate' in the prior action, we think it would be unfair in this case to use the prior result to the disadvantage of the defendant." This lack of incentive to litigate may take the form of a burdensome, lengthy trial or the lack of opportunity to call witnesses, as discussed by the court in the Parklane Hosiery case[112] that 1979 court nevertheless concluded that the defendants "had every incentive to litigate the prior SEC lawsuit fully and vigorously."[113]

Full opportunity to be heard, an essential element of res judicata, may involve such indicators as the amount of damages sought by the plaintiff, the seriousness of the allegations against the defendant, as well as the probability of future suits against the defendant. The Berner case[114] illustrates disproportionate damages as justifying denial of res judicata; here, after a fatal airplane crash, the defendant airline did not appeal an adverse judgment of $35,000 awarded to the estate of a deceased passenger, and subsequently another plaintiff suing for $7 million attempted to preclude the defendant airline on the issue of liability. The court denied preclusion because defendant's failure to appeal the first verdict proved that the defendant had not been motivated to contest liability vigorously in the first suit when only $35,000 was at stake. In contrast thereto was the decision in United States v. United Airlines, Inc.,[115] where the "first judgment involved 24 of 31 pending actions; the gravity of the potential liability is shown by the fact that the ultimate judgments against the air line totalled $2,237,308. . . . Obviously, the air line would have exerted its full efforts with so much at stake."[116]

Litigants who anticipate future suits tend to litigate more vigorously to avoid losing an issue which subsequently may be precluded.[117] As the Second U.S. Court of Appeals in Evergreens v. Nunan[118] observed: "Defeat in one suit might entail results beyond all calculation by either party; a trivial controversy might bring utter disaster in its train. There is no reason for subjecting the loser to such extravagant hazards. . . . "[119] Foreseeability of future suits is measured by an objective standard as shown in Zdanok v. Glidden Co.,[120] where the court applied preclusion against the defendant employer, who sought to relitigate the interpretation of an employment contract when a second group of employees sought recompense under the same contract of employment.

In examining whether there has been full and fair opportunity to be heard, the courts will observe such matters as the competence and experience of trial counsel in the prior action and the size of the prior claim compared to the size of the claim in the subsequent action. It was that latter inquiry into the "money difference" that featured in the ruling of the New York Court of Appeals in

Koch v. Consolidated Edison Co.[121] Here the court unanimously held that the defendant in the earlier case[122] (wherein the court assessed damages against the defendant in the sum of $40,500) had been given a ''full and fair opportunity to litigate the issue of gross negligence,'' and then ''recognizing the potential preclusive effects of an adverse determination . . . had every incentive to defend the action fully and vigorously.'' In the instant case, claims against the defendant amounted to $20 million, these claims arising out of the 1977 power ''blackout'' in New York City. The victorious plaintiff was the City of New York and Mayor Edward Koch.[123]

But an appellate court in New York earlier in 1975 in Vincent v. Thompson[124] had not accepted plaintiff's argument that collateral estoppel reduced the case to an issue of damages only. Here a child became ill following administration of the drug product Quadrigen vaccine, after an earlier court decision established that the product was defective and could cause the same injuries in others. The New York court observed that there were a variety of factors completely unrelated to the defect in the product, for, indeed, there may be factors in the instant plaintiff's background which could have changed the nature and the extent of the risk entirely.[125]

A smart defendant, however, had utilized the doctrine of collateral estoppel to his decided advantage, according to press reports of a deal made in Philadelphia in early 1982 between a winning plaintiff and the losing drug manufacturer. After settlement was agreed upon, the plaintiff joined with defendant in a request to the court for a new trial, the purpose being to expunge from the record the adverse verdict and the settlement. In essence, the court in granting the motion for a new trial gave effect to collateral estoppel.[126]

3.5 INCONSISTENT JUDGMENTS AND FULL FAITH AND CREDIT

The likelihood of inconsistent judgments which are given full faith and credit is another essential element of res judicata. In Desmond v. Kramer[127] the New Jersey court granted preclusion to an injured passenger on a bus who had not been a party to the first suit in which fourteen other passengers had won a favorable judgment. The court reasoned that the defendants had a full and fair opportunity to litigate since the original suit approximated a class action, and the prior verdicts would not be inconsistent: ''The problem of inconsistent verdicts can be avoided if, as a practical matter, a rule is adopted which would allow the application of Res Judicata only where there has been no actual inconsistency.''[128] In the Parklane Hosiery case[129] the U.S. Supreme Court opined that allowing preclusion may be ''unfair to a defendant if the judgment relied upon as a basis for the preclusion is itself inconsistent with one or more previous judgments in favor of the defendant.''

But the inconsistent judgments rule relies too heavily upon the first decision as being correct.[130] A judgment for the defendant in the first suit prevents subsequent plaintiffs from utilizing a later favorable judgment, although the defendant's liability will necessarily be relitigated in each subsequent suit. But a judgment for the plaintiff in the first suit will preclude the defendant on the issue of liability in all subsequent suits. Thus, the inconsistent judgments rule forces the defendant to present only one formidable defense in the first suit, and if defendant loses, he will be subsequently precluded from relitigating that issue; if defendant wins, the defendant may later defend in the normal manner without fear of future issue preclusions.

Article IV, Section 1 of the U.S. Constitution states that "Full Faith and Credit shall be given in each State to the public Acts, Records and judicial Proceedings of every other State." And 28 USC 1738 affirms that "the records and judicial proceedings of any court of any . . . State, Territory, or Possession . . . or copies thereof, so authenticated, shall have the same full faith and credit in every court within the United States and its Territories and Possessions as they have by law or usage in the courts of such State, Territory, or Possession from which they are taken." Thus, the res judicata effect of a judgment is respected in every court within the United States, and the inconsistent judgment rule is thus observed in terms of preclusion.

In the international field the possibility of inconsistent judgments is also of prime concern, but there are more paramount considerations of political significance as well as social and economic considerations. In China Trade and Development Corp. v. M. V. Chong Yong (——F Supp——[SDNY, Sept. 1987]), the federal district court for the Southern District of New York, in an opinion by Judge Motley, enjoined in 1987 the defendants from proceeding with a parallel action instituted in South Korea two and a half years after suit was commenced in the federal district court. Judge Motley observed that, while "courts have the power to enjoin litigants from pursuing simultaneous contests in a foreign forum, . . . comity militates against granting such relief, since the issuance of an injunction can deprive the other country in which suit is instituted of its sovereignty to some extent." But Judge Motley was willing to take that bold step here of shutting off the South Korea action because (a) the parties were identical, and (b) the resolution of the federal district court action was dispositive of the action to be enjoined. Furthermore, the court had fully considered such factors as "(1) frustration of a policy in the enjoining forum; (2) the foreign action would be vexatious; (3) a threat to the issuing court's in rem or quasi in rem jurisdiction; (4) the proceedings in the other forum prejudice other equitable considerations; or (5) adjudication of the same issue in separate actions would result in delay, inconvenience, expense, inconsistency, or a race to judgment." The federal district court stressed the fact that pursuit of the South Korea action would be "vexatious" to plaintiffs since defendants had waited two and a half years to commence suit in South Korea!

4

Essential Elements of Collateral Estoppel: Preclusion by Prior Adjudication

Collateral estoppel is perhaps an aspect of res judicata or even a corollary to the rule of res judicata,[131] but collateral estoppel has an existence of its own. The classic definition appeared in the 1876 U.S. Supreme Court decision of Cromwell v. County of Sac: ''Where the second action between the same parties is upon a different claim or demand, the judgment in the prior action operates as an estoppel only as to those matters in issue or points controverted, upon the determination of which the finding or verdict was rendered. . . . Only upon such matters is the judgment conclusive in another action.''[132] Simply put, collateral estoppel is issue or fact preclusion, as opposed to res judicata, which is claim or cause of action preclusion.[133] Historically, collateral estoppel was incorporated into English common law as ''estoppel by record'': in Outram v. Morewood[134] the plaintiff sued a husband and wife in trespass for mining coal on property of which plaintiff claimed ownership; defendants entered a plea averring that the wife had obtained the land in question by a devise from her first husband. Plaintiff replied by requesting ''estoppel by record,'' and Lord Ellenbourough observed that

> it is not the recovery, but the matter alleged by the party, and upon which the recovery proceeds, which creates the estoppel. The recovery of itself in an action of trespass is only a bar to future recovery of damages for the same injury; but the estoppel precludes parties and privies from contending to the contrary of that point, or matter of fact, which having once been distinctly put in issue by them . . . has been, on such issue joined, solemnly found against them.[135]

Professor Miller in 1940 pointed out that the basis for the preclusion by estoppel "was not the judgment qua judgment, . . . but the process . . . the pleadings and verdict, as authenticated by the judgment, and by virtue not of Res Judicata but of the restraint upon contradiction of the previous record involved in the idea of estoppel."[136] Indeed, according to Miller, "estoppel by record," "estoppel by deed," and "estoppel in pais," predecessors of collateral estoppel, contain a recognition that by actions or assertions in the prior case "the party had created or participated in creating a condition from which the law would not suffer him to recede."[137]

It is said that collateral estoppel sweeps further than res judicata in the sense that the former application is not restricted to later suits between the same parties and their privies; only the party against whom the doctrine of collateral estoppel is invoked must have been present or represented in the prior action.[138] But the principle of mutuality[139] prevented any party from benefiting from an estoppel unless that party could also be burdened by it; indeed, mutuality limited the scope of collateral estoppel to situations where the parties in the second suit were either opposing parties or in privity with opposing parties in the first suit.[140] However, res judicata has a more extensive effect than collateral estoppel in that res judicata may be applied to bar claims or causes of action that could have been but were not litigated in the prior suit.[141]

In determining the availability of collateral estoppel courts have taken into consideration such essential elements as (1) identity of parties; (2) identical issues or facts; (3) validity and finality of the judgment or award; (4) full opportunity to be heard; (5) inconsistent judgments and full faith and credit; (6) changed circumstances and/or advances in scientific knowledge; (7) the substantive or procedural law of the forum; and (8) whether the doctrine of collateral estoppel is utilized offensively or defensively,[142] all of which are delineated hereinafter in Chapters 4 and 5.

4.1 IDENTITY OF PARTIES AND COLLATERAL ESTOPPEL

The successful utilization of collateral estoppel depends upon many essential elements set forth hereinafter, but the starting point is the determination of the identity of the parties against whom and for whom the doctrine should apply. If the party asserting collateral estoppel and the party against whom the doctrine is applied are both bound by the prior judgment, collateral estoppel clearly applies. This principle of mutuality simply requires that the parties in the second suit be the same or be in privity with the parties in the first suit, and therefore be bound by the prior judgment. The difficulty arises when a nonparty in the first suit, a stranger to the prior judgment, attempts to prevent the relitigation of an issue or fact in the second suit. "Defensive use" of collateral estoppel occurs when a stranger to the prior judgment asserts the prior judgment as a "shield" against the plaintiff who was a party to the first suit. "Offensive use" of collateral estoppel occurs where a plaintiff who is a stranger to the first suit seeks to assert the prior judgment as a "sword" against the defendant who is bound by the prior judgment.[143]

But a prior determination may bind one who stands in a special relationship to a party to the prior proceeding, and that relationship is usually termed one of privity.[144] Unfortunately, the definition of "privity" is dependent upon what a given court observes on a given day, i.e., the court has reached the legal conclusion that the relationship of the party in question is such that the preclusive doctrine of collateral estoppel should apply.[145] Parties in privity may have a "concurrent" relationship, a "successive" relationship, or a "representation of the interests of the same person."[146] Like the concept of privity, the principle of mutuality requires a special relationship of the party involving collateral estoppel; and mutuality is based on equality of opportunity that "would deny to one party an appropriate right or remedy because the corresponding right or remedy is not available to, or appropriate for, his adversary."[147] Thus, a party cannot benefit from the invocation of a prior judgment unless he was bound thereby. Less than one-fourth of the states follow the principle of mutuality today,[148] especially after the California Supreme Court in 1942 led a major assault on mutuality, as Judge Traynor could find no justification for the requirement that a party invoking collateral estoppel had to be bound by the prior adjudication.[149] The thrust of that 1942 decision was simply that a party who had an opportunity to litigate his claim should not be presented with a second chance. The U.S. Supreme Court in 1971 in Blonder-Tongue Laboratories, Inc. v. University of Illinois Foundation[150] abolished the requirement of mutuality.

The minority view supporting mutuality is seen in the Ohio decision of Goodson v. McDonough Power Equipment, Inc.,[151] a products liability situation based upon an alleged design defect. The minor plaintiff suffered injuries as a result of a lawnmower manufactured by the defendant; the accident occurred while the infant was given a ride on the lawnmower despite warnings to the contrary. Another plaintiff running alongside the lawnmower had to have her left foot amputated. Plaintiffs' contention pointed to the lack of a safety guard, and plaintiff moved to preclude the defendant from relitigating the issue of negligent product design based upon a 1974 decision of a federal district court in Florida in which the defendant was the defendant therein.[152] In that earlier case a minor plaintiff's foot had to be amputated allegedly due to the faulty design of the lawnmower and its lack of a safety guard. The Ohio trial court in the instant case ruled that the doctrine of collateral estoppel could be invoked to prevent the defendant from relitigating the issue of its negligence, and judgment for the plaintiffs was entered on the issue of liability. But the Ohio Court of Appeals in 1983 reversed, holding that the trial court had improperly granted a summary judgment in the face of a disputed material fact, although the appellate court did not reject the application of collateral estoppel. The Ohio Supreme Court reversed, pointing out that collateral estoppel should not be invoked in cases involving defective design of mass-produced products where the issues and adjudications arose out of "separate underlying incidents."[153] The highest Ohio court observed the absence of mutuality in that the plaintiffs here were not parties to the earlier proceedings, nor were they in privity with the plaintiffs in the earlier proceedings. And since the present plaintiffs would not have been bound by a decision adverse to the plaintiffs in the earlier proceedings, they could not assert a favorable decision to preclude litigation by the defendant here: "In our opinion, the existing Ohio requirement that there be an identity of parties or their privies is founded upon the sound principle that all persons are entitled to their day in court."[154] Another concern voiced by the highest Ohio court was that the excessive cost of satisfying due process requirements where mutuality was lacking would eliminate any benefit gained in terms of judicial economy.[155]

Joinder describes procedural methods of unifying parties; plaintiffs may join in one action if they raise a common question in asserting a right to relief arising out of the same transaction or occurrence. But where a non-party "could easily have joined" in the first action but did not do so, he is not later entitled to the benefit of the earlier judgment, as stated by the U.S. Supreme Court in the Parklane Hosiery case.[156] Section 88 (3) of Restatement (Second) of Judgments denies collateral estoppel if the party asserting it "could have effected joinder in the first action between himself and his present adversary."[157] The joinder rule is useful in preventing any unfairness that might result: (1) a defendant, fearing an unfavorable verdict that multiple plaintiffs may use later, may feel compelled in the first suit to make a settlement which has no estoppel effect; the joinder rule reduces any compulsion for a defendant to settle unsatisfactorily; (2) plaintiffs might be tempted to arrange the order of trials so that the most badly injured or the most sympathetic plaintiff will try his case first; the joinder rule discourages such collusion because subsequent plaintiffs who could readily have joined cannot use the original judgment; and (3) a plaintiff should not be permitted to ignore the public interest in minimizing litigation by avoiding joinder and later use to his advantage the judgment in the suit that he avoided joining. But a leading case approving the application of collateral estoppel where fellow employees failed to join the initial lawsuit and where the prior determination against the employer was binding upon the employer is Zdanok v. Glidden Co.[158] The Second U.S. Court of Appeals pointed out here that the employer's opportunity to litigate the first case was both full and fair; that New York was an entirely reasonable forum for litigation of an employment contract made in New York with respect to New York residents working in a New York plant; and that the employer could not reasonably argue that it was unfairly surprised by the entry of the new plaintiffs after the adverse judgment in the first suit. However, in Albernaz v. Fall River[159] the Massachusetts court held that a decree allowing city employees increased salaries did not preclude the city from relitigating the question of its liability under that decree in a subsequent suit brought by other employees of the city who were neither parties nor privies to parties in the first suit.

4.2 IDENTICAL ISSUES OR FACTS AND COLLATERAL ESTOPPEL

Another essential element of collateral estoppel is the necessity of identical issues or facts, as illustrated by Loundsbury v. Keene:[160] here the town had lost a suit to enforce a sign ordinance against a local bank whose sign predated the ordinance, but the New Hampshire court in a subsequent suit by the town against another party would not apply collateral estoppel since the issue in the first case was whether the bank had a vested interest or vested right to maintain the sign, which was not a safety hazard and was aesthetically pleasing, and since the issue in the second case was whether a sign owner had a vested interest or vested right to maintain a sign that the town considered aesthetically undesirable. In short, there was no identity of issues. But in In Re Falstaff Corp. Antitrust Litigation[161] new defendants could invoke collateral estoppel against the plaintiff as to issues in securities regulations where the factual issues were identical and grew out of the same transaction. In Borough of Lansdale v. Federal Power Commission[162] the court asserted that "a party asserting Collateral Estoppel has the burden of showing identity of issues and determination of issues on the merits"; it was not sufficient to introduce merely the decision of the prior court unless an adequate record pinpointing the exact issues litigated is produced.[163] The New York Court of Appeals in Schwartz v. Public Administrator[164] emphasized that there must be identity of issues necessarily decided in the prior action and decisive of the present litigation.

The U.S. Supreme Court in the Blonder-Tongue case[165] stressed considerations of judicial economy and freedom from vexatious litigation:

> In any lawsuit where a defendant . . . is forced to present a complete defense on the merits to a claim where the plaintiff has fully litigated and lost in a prior action, there is an arguable misallocation of resources. To the extent that the defendant in the second suit may not win by asserting, without contradiction, that the plaintiff had fully and fairly, but unsuccessfully, litigated the same claim in the prior suit, the defendant's time and money are diverted from alternative uses, productive or otherwise, to relitigation of a decided issue. And still, assuming that the issue was resolved correctly in the first suit, there is reason to be concerned about the plaintiff's allocation of resources. Permitting repeated litigation of the same issue as long as the supply of unrelated defendants holds out reflects either the aura of the gaming table or "a lack of discipline and of disinterestedness on the part of the lower courts, hardly a worthy or wise basis for fashioning rules of procedure."[166]

4.3 VALIDITY AND FINALITY OF JUDGMENT OR AWARD

A basic objective of collateral estoppel is judicial finality, a valid and final judgment or award.[167] Indeed, the finality of a valid judicial determination is an expectation of the community, for it serves the needs of society by focusing upon the efficient administration of justice and the maintenance of the courts as prestigious and honorable institutions. Both society and the courts are interested also in the settlement or the finality of the differences between the parties to the dispute.[168] The U.S. Supreme Court in 1877 expressed the concept in these terms: "It is a finality as to the claim or demand in controversy, concluding parties and those in privity with them, not only as to every matter which was offered and received to sustain or defeat the claim or demand, but as to any other admissible matter which might have been offered for that purpose."[169]

But this air or purpose of finality is not necessarily summum bonum, as illustrated by Hardy v. Johns-Manville Sales Corp.,[170] where the Fifth U.S. Court of Appeals ruled that the plaintiffs may not rely on the finality of the 1974 court's earlier decision in Borel v. Fibreboard Paper Products Corp.[171] because (a) there were ambiguities as to precisely what issues were "necessarily decided" by the jury in the Borel case; (b) the verdict in the Borel case was actually inconsistent with subsequent judgments in favor of the defendants; and (c) it is doubtful that the defendants in the Borel case could have foreseen the staggering dimensions of their potential liability in the years after 1974.

4.4 FULL AND FAIR OPPORTUNITY TO BE HEARD

The essential element of full and fair opportunity to be heard is fundamentally one of fairness and equity, for no person should be bound by a prior determination if he had not the full opportunity to be heard or to litigate the matter. The application of collateral estoppel here is entirely within the discretion of the trial court.[172] Among the countless factors that a trial court might consider as determinative of whether a party has had a full and fair opportunity to be heard are the following: the size of the claims, the forum of the prior litigation, the use of initiative, the extent of the litigation, the competence and experience of trial counsel, the availability of new evidence, the indications of a compromise verdict or judgment, differences in the applicable law, and the foreseeability of future litigation.[173]

In an action against a bank for fraudently conspiring to induce plaintiff to enter into a partnership and become liable to the bank on a note, the federal district court in Wyoming permitted the bank to invoke collateral estoppel against the plaintiff since plaintiff had a full and fair opportunity and incentive to litigate vigorously the issues in a prior action.[174] But whether or not a party had a full and fair opportunity to be heard is difficult to resolve; if a party knows or has reason to fear that an adverse decision will be utilized by non-parties to the first suit, he may very well proceed with great vigor but with a minimum of expense if he is certain that his exposure to liability is only minimal, and yet an adverse decision for minimal damages might collaterally estop him from relitigating the issue or the facts in a subsequent suit for greater damages.[175]

In DiOrio v. Scottsdale[176] the Arizona court had occasion to remark that "it is generally accepted that a party who has had one full and fair opportunity to prove a claim in a court of competent jurisdiction and has failed to do so, should not be permitted to go to trial on the merits of that claim a second time. Both orderliness and reasonable time saving of judicial administration require that this be so. . . . ''[177] Five years later in 1970 the Fifth U.S. Court of Appeals emphasized that

> the doctrine of Collateral Estoppel will not be applied unless it appears that the party against whom the estoppel is asserted had a full and fair opportunity to litigate the issue in the prior proceeding, and that the application of the doctrine will not result in an injustice to the party against whom it is asserted under the particular circumstances of the case.[178]

4.5 INCONSISTENT JUDGMENTS AND FULL FAITH AND CREDIT

Another essential element of collateral estoppel is the lack of inconsistent judgments, i.e., collateral estoppel effect is denied to findings that are inconsistent with earlier findings.[179] The rationale is that if two courts reach conflicting determinations, the question must be sufficiently close or intractable to dispel confidence in either determination. Nevertheless, some courts have observed that retrial of issues previously determined might embarrass the judicial system were the second court to reach contrary results.[180] If the reliability of findings made in the first suit is in doubt, it might be more embarrassing to the judicial system to give these findings preclusive effect in a second suit. On the other hand, collateral estoppel has been applied in some cases to prevent inconsistent judgments that might undermine the integrity of the judicial system,[181] which depends upon a widespread belief that all or most decisions are reliable. In deciding whether or not to apply collateral estoppel a court must seek assurances that specific determinations, adequate for the purposes of a single case, are sufficiently reliable to bind a litigant in a second or third or fourth suit.[182]

In the Parklane Hosiery case[183] the highest court cited ''inconsistent judgments'' as a further justification for its holding; in Borel v. Fibreboard Paper Products Co.[184] the court, while admitting that inconsistent judgments per se will not defeat collateral estoppel (since the defendant may have prevailed due to plaintiff's failure to establish causation), stated: ''A court able to say that the approximately 35 suits decided in favor of asbestos manufacturers were all decided on the basis of insufficient exposure on the part of the plaintiff or the failure to demonstrate an asbestos-related disease, would be clairvoyant.''[185] Multiple litigation may indeed subject any defendant to judgments that conflict on the issue of liability, and the possibility of inconsistent judgments is best seen in mass accidents where nearly every victim files an individual claim or is part of a class action on the identical issue. In a 1958 case California rejected multiple plaintiff estoppel, denying the plaintiff parents of an infant passenger the use of the infant's judgment to establish the negligence of a common defendant.[186] The California appellate court excluded "multiple claims of different persons for personal injuries or property damage against a single defendant or set of defendants growing out of a single accident"[187] from the application of the rule abandoning mutuality of persons.[188] The New Jersey court in Reardon v. Allen[189] denied collateral estoppel to multiple plaintiffs to utilize a prior determination of negligence in an automobile collision because inconsistent judgments were possible.

Where the prior judgment was the product of a jury compromise and therefore tainted, courts will deny the application of collateral estoppel, as illustrated by Katz v. Eli Lilly & Co.,[190] in the subsequent suit by another plaintiff or plaintiffs.

Collateral estoppel has been applied in the international field so as to give recognition and enforcement to foreign judgments in the United States, as illustrated by Sorman-Braunstein v. Braunstein,[191] where the New York court viewed a Swedish divorce proceeding awarding child custody to the wife and ordering the husband to pay child maintenance; the winning wife sought distribution of marital property located in New York as well as further child support and insurance. The New York court examined the Swedish judgment and found it to be "seemingly conducted in accordance with fair procedures," i.e., the Swedish court had personal jurisdiction over the parties, who were both represented by counsel, inter alia. The New York court determined that "the parties to an action are collaterally estopped from relitigating an issue decided in a prior proceeding when they have had a full and fair opportunity to be heard on that issue."[192] Collateral estoppel has also been given effect with respect to crucial, ultimate facts necessarily determined in prior foreign litigation,[193] but has been denied application when the foreign suit involved property different from that at issue in the U.S. litigation,[194] or when the defendant was not a party nor a privy to the foreign suit.[195] Indeed, U.S. courts will generally afford collateral estoppel effect to foreign judgments in proper circumstances.[196]

Full faith and credit is embodied in Section 450 (2) of Restatement of Conflict of Laws to the effect that "the law of the state where the judgment was rendered" determines "the effect of a valid judgment as a conclusive adjudication between the parties and persons in privity with them, of the facts which were or might have been put in issue." In Harnischfeger Sales Corp. v. Sternberg Dredging Co.[197] a nonresident made a limited appearance in Louisiana to defend a dredge claim and litigated issues arising out of its purchase. Even though the Louisiana judgment had the limited effect of a quasi-in-rem judgment in that it disposed of the dredge but did not merge the plaintiff's cause of action, the judgment was held, in a subsequent suit between the parties in Mississippi for the balance of the purchase price, to have a collateral estoppel effect as to the facts litigated.[198]

4.6 CHANGED CIRCUMSTANCES AND/OR ADVANCES IN SCIENTIFIC KNOWLEDGE

A number of cases have recognized that the application of collateral estoppel is improper where there are changed circumstances or advances in scientific knowledge between the date of the first judgment and the subsequent litigation.[199] The rationale is that intervening factual change can displace a fact or issue on which the initial judgment depended. The U.S. Supreme Court in 1948 declared: "Collateral Estoppel is designed to prevent repetitious lawsuits over matters which have once been decided and which have remained substantially static, factually and legally. It is not meant to create vested rights in decisions that have become obsolete or erroneous with time. . . ."[200]

In the products liability field collateral estoppel has been defeated by defendants introducing new scientific developments which threw doubt on the theories of causation relied upon in prior cases.[201]

4.7 SUBSTANTIVE OR PROCEDURAL LAW OF THE FORUM

In the first and last analysis the applicability of collateral estoppel focuses upon the substantive law of the state in which the subsequent action is brought. Since about one-fourth of the states have not abandoned the mutuality requirement, the choice of the forum state for the subsequent suit may be a most significant factor. The query is complicated by the fact that collateral estoppel is substantive in some states and procedural in other states. In Hardy v. Johns-Manville Sales Corp.,[202] for example, the Fifth U.S. Court of Appeals applied the federal law of collateral estoppel despite the court's acknowledgment that the forum state of Texas required mutuality of parties. In Amader v. Johns-Manville Sales Corp.[203] the federal district court in Pennsylvania contended that federal courts should apply the forum state's substantive law when adjudicating diversity cases: "State collateral estoppel rules when adjudicating diversity cases. State collateral rules are substantive." A New Jersey court in Mayor of Paterson v. Baker[204] stressed that

> Collateral Estoppel is not a mere rule of procedure, limited in its operation, and only to be enforced in cases where a defeated suitor attempts to litigate anew a question once heard and decided against him, but a rule of justice, unlimited in its operation, which must be enforced whenever its enforcement is necessary for the protection and security of rights, and for the preservation of the repose of society.[205]

In an action to surcharge an executor of an estate for payment of real estate commissions, the executor was collaterally estopped in In Re Estate of Ellis[206] from alleging that there was no contractual relationship between the executor and the realtor, where the realtor had previously been awarded a commission on the sale of the property and an appeal of that award had been filed by the executor but withdrawn.

In recent years, however, there has been a detachment of collateral estoppel from substantive or vested rights as the courts commenced to exercise more discretionary roles and give the judicial system greater flexibility. Modern collateral estoppel is recognized as a procedural interest, not a vested substantive right, of a prevailing party not to be required to relitigate an issue previously determined in his favor. Similarly, there is recognized a public interest in avoiding the costs of repetitious adjudication. The U.S. Supreme Court in 1978 in the Parklane Hosiery Co. case[207] lent important impetus to the trend toward investing collateral estoppel with the raiment of equitable discretion.

5

Offensive Collateral Estoppel v. Defensive Collateral Estoppel

Collateral estoppel may be pleaded in two different ways where the parties are not identical.[208] ''Offensive'' utilization occurs where a plaintiff who is a stranger or a non-party to the first suit seeks to assert collateral estoppel as a ''sword'' against the defendant who lost the prior judgment and is bound by the prior judgment. ''Defensive'' utilization occurs where a defendant who is a stranger or a non-party to the first suit asserts the prior judgment as a ''shield'' against the plaintiff who was a party to the first suit. In both situations the party who is asserting collateral estoppel is a stranger or non-party to the prior judgment and therefore not bound by the prior judgment, but he seeks to assert the judgment against the party who is bound by the prior judgment. Obviously, in those twelve or more states[209] adhering to the rule of mutuality of parties, neither offensive nor defensive collateral estoppel would be applicable since the party asserting collateral estoppel is himself not bound by the prior judgment.[210] A stranger or non-party to the prior judgment, having ''no legal right to defend or control the proceedings, nor to appeal from the decree,''[211] was not bound and could not invoke the prior judgment to prevent relitigation of an issue or fact previously determined by a court.

Thus, collateral estoppel may be used offensively or defensively. Where a losing party in the first suit becomes a defendant in a subsequent suit, plaintiffs who were not parties in the first suit may use collateral estoppel offensively to preclude the former losing party from relitigating issues or facts that have already been decided against it.[212] Defensive collateral estoppel occurs where a party that has lost an action becomes a plaintiff in a subsequent suit and seeks a redetermination of an issue or fact decided adversely to it in the prior suit; the new defendant may collaterally estop the plaintiff, as illustrated by Oldham v. Pritchett,[213] where the issue of the driver's negligence had been litigated in the prior suit so that a passenger who sued the driver of the boat in the subsequent suit was collaterally estopped because the passenger had an opportunity to introduce evidence regarding the driver's comparative or contributory negligence in the prior suit.

It is frequently stated that collateral estoppel invariably saves both courts and litigants time and money, and prevents harassment of individuals who have already expended both time and money in the first suit.[214] This economy rationale does comport with the defensive utilization of collateral estoppel, for when a party prevents an adversary from relitigating issues or facts decided in the prior suit, he indirectly fosters judicial economy. On the other hand, offensive utilization of collateral estoppel does not necessarily prevent the harassment that can flow from repetitive litigation; prospective plaintiffs are encouraged to bring suits that otherwise might not be brought. Furthermore, the potential application of offensive collateral estoppel can encourage a prospective plaintiff to await a future suit rather than intervene now in a pending suit. As the U.S. Supreme Court expressed it in the Parklane Hosiery Co. case[215]

> Since a plaintiff will be able to rely on a previous judgment against a defendant but will not be bound by that judgment if the defendant wins, the plaintiff has every incentive to adopt a "wait and see" attitude, in the hope that the first action by another plaintiff will result in a favorable judgment. . . . Thus, offensive use of collateral estoppel will likely increase rather than decrease the total amount of litigation, since potential plaintiffs will have everything to gain and nothing to lose by not intervening in the first action.[216]

Offensive collateral estoppel may also be criticized as extending the reach of some unreliable judgments in those cases where the losing party did not vigorously defend the first suit for a variety of logical reasons.[217]

5.1 OFFENSIVE COLLATERAL ESTOPPEL

One Leo Shore filed a class action suit against Parklane Hosiery Co., Inc., in the federal district court for the Southern District of New York, alleging that defendant had violated certain sections of the Securities and Exchange Act.[218] Before the suit came to trial the Securities and Exchange Commission filed suit against the same defendant seeking injunctive relief based upon the same issue of a materially false and misleading proxy statement. The SEC action resulted in a finding that defendant was at fault, and that judgment was affirmed by the Second U.S. Court of Appeals.[219] Shore thereupon claimed that defendant was collaterally estopped from relitigating the falsity and misleading nature of the proxy statement, and he moved for summary judgment, but the court denied the motion on the ground that the defendant had a Seventh Amendment right to a jury trial on that issue. The Second U.S. Court of Appeals reversed,[220] holding that the defendant had a full and fair opportunity[221] to litigate that issue in the prior non-jury trial. The U.S. Supreme Court affirmed,[222] giving birth to a full-scale recognition of offensive collateral estoppel, although the court did set forth two caveats, to wit: offensive and collateral estoppel should not be allowed when either the plaintiff could have easily joined in the prior suit, or the court determines that estoppel would be unfair to the defendant. In the instant case, it should be noted, the plaintiff could not join the prior action because such joinder was prohibited by statute.[223] Furthermore, the application of offensive collateral estoppel here was deemed not to be unfair to the defendant, who had every opportunity to litigate fully and fairly the particular issue in the prior suit brought by the SEC.

The highest court also pointed out that proper use of offensive collateral estoppel does not violate the right to a jury trial under the Seventh Amendment. Earlier in Galloway v. United States[224] the same court wrote that the Seventh Amendment "was designed to preserve the basic institution of jury trial in only its most fundamental elements, not the great mass of procedural forms and details varying then even so widely among common law jurisdictions."[225] Later, in Beacon Theatres v. Westover,[226] the highest court held that legal jurisdiction and its concomitant right to a jury trial can be determined by the present-day adequacy of the legal remedy. And in Atlas Roofing Co. v. OSHA,[227] where plaintiffs protested the determination of a fine in an administrative hearing, claiming that the Seventh Admendment entitled them to a jury trial, the highest court disagreed and held that "in cases in which 'public rights' are being litigated, e.g., cases in which the Government sues in its sovereign capacity to enforce public rights created by statute, the Seventh Amendment does not require a jury trial."[228]

Offensive collateral estoppel is somewhat plagued by the complications arising out of changes in strategy, evidence, cross-examination, and overall techniques of trial that a jury may in fact be presented with different issues between the first suit and the subsequent suit, as illustrated by State Farm Fire & Casualty Co. v. Century Home Components, Inc.[229] Here a fire in a sawdust box in defendant's lumber yard spread to nearby property, causing property damages to several plaintiffs. The first suit resulted in a verdict for defendant.[230] A second suit against the same defendant alleged that the fire was caused by spontaneous combustion, but the defense won again based upon the argument that children in the neighborhood might have caused the fire since they were responsible for a similar fire earlier that evening.[231] After other suits were filed the plaintiffs changed strategy to emphasize that defendant was simply negligent in maintaining the sawdust box where the fire started, and this change of strategy undercut defendant's defense evidence about the boys' responsibility for the fire. Deciding whether there was an unreasonable risk of spontaneous combustion is substantially different from deciding whether there was reasonable care of the premises in light of the prior incidents of fires. Thus, the verdicts were not inconsistent and did not preclude offensive collateral estoppel on the issue of liability.[232] In Mooney v. Fibreboard Corp.[233] plaintiff employee sued eleven corporations on a theory of strict liability seeking damages for his asbestosis, and argued that he was entitled to offensive collateral estoppel against the defendant asbestos manufacturer on the issue of the defective and unreasonably dangerous product. Seven years earlier in Borel v. Fibreboard Paper Products Corp.[234] the Fifth U.S. Court of Appeals had affirmed a judgment upon a jury finding that asbestos products were unreasonably dangerous and defective. Six of the eleven defendants in the instant case had been defendants in the Borel case, and four had settled their cases prior to judgment; only the eleventh defendant had no connection with the Borel case. Plaintiff here argued that a majority of the named defendants here had a full and fair opportunity to litigate the issue of product defect in the first case, and accordingly should be estopped from relitigating that issue in this subsequent suit. The federal district court in Texas found that an ''asbestosis case, like many other mass torts . . . is an appropriate candidate for the offensive use of collateral estoppel,''[235] and the court estopped the six defendants who had been parties in the Borel case. The defendants had argued that they should not be estopped because other asbestosis cases had gone to judgment in defendants' favor, to which the court replied: ''To follow defendants' reasoning, one frivolous lawsuit would preclude courts from using modern principles of collateral estoppel in cases where an issue had clearly been determined adversely to a defendant in other actions.''[236] It is interesting to note that the federal district court in Mississippi in 1980 had cited twenty-four asbestos cases of which fourteen were decided in favor of defendants![237] In this 1980 case the plaintiffs were unsuccessful in asserting offensive collateral estoppel against the defendants, as the federal district court held that Mississippi law adhered to the doctrine of mutuality of parties and the defendants who were not parties to the earlier cited cases could not therefore be bound thereby:

> If collateral estoppel was applied . . . the court would have no alternative but to bifurcate the trial, and this would lead the court to apply different standards of proof as to the different groups of defendants, would no doubt confuse the jury, and would present issues to be tried as to each different group of defendants. Clearly, judicial economy would not be served, and such a procedure would be patently unfair to . . . defendants.[238]

A federal district court in Missouri the same year expressed similar thinking: ''Allowing Offensive Collateral Estoppel may also be unfair to a defendant if judgment relied upon as a basis for estoppel is itself inconsistent with one or more previous judgments in favor of defendant.''[239]

Under the Federal Racketeer Influenced and Corrupt Organizations Act, or

RICO,[240] Section 1964 (d) provides that "a final judgment or decree rendered in favor of the United States in any criminal proceeding brought by the United States under this chapter shall estop the defendant from denying the essential allegations of the criminal offense in any subsequent civil proceeding brought by the United States." This example of offensive collateral estoppel precludes a defendant from contesting the racketeering activity which has been alleged against him in a civil RICO suit where that defendant has previously pleaded guilty or been convicted of the same criminal charge.

5.2 DEFENSIVE COLLATERAL ESTOPPEL

It is said that defensive collateral estoppel tends to decrease the amount of litigation by preventing a plaintiff from relitigating identical issues by merely switching adversaries, for example. In the products liability field defensive collateral estoppel seems to have little play unless the losing defendant seeks to estop the plaintiff from asserting an issue or fact which had previously been litigated unsuccessfully, as illustrated by Pennington v. Snow,[241] where the Alaska Supreme Court denied the defensive collateral estoppel because the particular circumstances of the prior adjudication made it unfair to give the first judgment conclusive force. Here two suits were instituted by the plaintiffs, husband and wife, in courts of differing jurisdictions. In the superior court they sought $175,000, alleging that defendant's negligence had caused the wife to miscarry. Simultaneously a claim by the husband in the district court against his insurance company for medical expenses terminated in favor of the carrier as the court found no causal relation between the accident and the miscarriage. When the defendant in the second suit sought to invoke defensive collateral estoppel, the Alaska Supreme Court refused to allow that defendant in the second suit to assert the prior judgment in favor of the insurance company as binding on the issue of causation in the second suit. According to the court, the plaintiff husband had not, by his choice of an expeditious result in the district court of a case of far less import, chosen the court in which to resolve all claims arising from the accident. In simple terms, the plaintiff did not have a full and fair opportunity to litigate his present claim in the prior action.[242] In this instance defensive collateral estoppel did not decrease the litigation, for the plaintiff was entitled to a full and fair opportunity to be heard.

In Spettigue v. Mahoney[243] the Arizona court considered the application of defensive collateral estoppel in a case where there was no unfairness since the party had had a prior full and fair opportunity to litigate the issue. While the court recognized that it is in the best public interest to preserve finality of litigation, the court poignantly observed that the party against whom the defensive collateral estoppel would be applied could not have been bound by the prior determination of that issue in the prior suit; and therefore the court refused to invoke estoppel. In essence, nonmutuality in defensive collateral estoppel would increase litigation in that it would give the parties an incentive to litigate their claims more fully and more expensively in the original suit, and also would create new issues in the subsequent suit concerning the question of whether collateral estoppel will be applied by the court against the present adversary.[244]

Defensive collateral estoppel was applied in Sanderson v. Balfour[245] by the New Hampshire Supreme Court. The plaintiff was the operator of a tractor which collided with a parked automobile operated by a wife as bailee of her husband. The present action was brought against her by the plaintiff for his personal injuries. The defendant wife pleaded collateral estoppel by a judgment in favor of her husband as to the negligence of the plaintiff in a suit successfully brought by the husband of the present defendant. Sustaining the wife's exception to the trial court's denial of her motion to dismiss on the ground of collateral estoppel, the New Hampshire Supreme Court recognized that this denial was in accord with the necessity of mutuality, but rested its decision on the fact that the plaintiff had a full and fair opportunity to be heard or to litigate the issue of his own negligence.

In Ellis v. Crockett[246] the purchasers of land and one of their creditors sued the vendors, claiming that defendants falsely and fraudulently failed to disclose who actually held the purchase note and mortgage on the day when the vendor's attorney demanded accelerated payment. The Hawaii Supreme Court, viewing the court record in a former foreclosure proceeding in which foreclosure was granted in favor of the vendors, opined that the present plaintiffs were precluded from litigating the fact of reassignment or any claim that would depend upon a finding that no reassignment had occurred.

On the other hand, defensive collateral estoppel was denied in Young & Co. v. Shea,[247] involving a longshoreman in a compensation hearing; the Fifth U.S. Court of Appeals ignored the prior proceeding in which it was determined that he sustained no injury because the court was influenced by the difference in procedural and evidentiary rules followed in the two proceedings and by the fact that all doubts in the subsequent compensation hearing were to be resolved in favor of the injured employee-longshoreman.

In a medical malpractice action brought by a minor against the hospital, after the minor sued both drivers involved in the accident which resulted in the minor's injuries and which claim was settled after judgment had been rendered, the minor's settlement was deemed by the Missouri appellate court not to support summary judgment in favor of the defendant by collateral estoppel because the record in prior proceedings indicated that settlement was entered into merely to collect the maximum amount of limited insurance coverage; the issue of liability of the instant defendant and full compensation for the plaintiff were simply not determined by the prior suit.[248]

6

Non-party Litigants and Due Process Limitations on Application of Res Judicata and Collateral Estoppel

The infamous case of Caulfield v. Fidelity & Casualty Co.[249] involved forty-two relatives of people buried in a Louisiana cemetery whose owner had cleared the land of brush and overgrowth and otherwise desecrated the cemetery. A total of twenty-nine separate but identical actions were filed, and all forty-two plaintiffs were represented by the same attorney. Suits were filed in two different Louisiana state district courts, and two of these state suits were removed to the federal district court. One state court case was tried first before a state jury and resulted in a verdict for the defendant cemetery owner. The federal court then ruled that the plaintiffs in the two actions pending before it were bound by that state judgment, and the Fifth U.S. Court of Appeals affirmed, relying on the Louisiana doctrine of judicial estoppel and declaring that precluding the other forty-one plaintiffs would ''prevent fruitless relitigation of an issue which already has been judicially determined'' and that ''absolutely nothing would be gained were appellants permitted to pursue their action.''[250] This incredible generalization that all forty-two plaintiffs were entitled to but ''one bite of the apple'' ignored the concepts of lack of privity and, most important, the mandate of due process of law, although concededly due process rights may be waived and the other forty-one plaintiffs could waive their rights to a day in court.[251] Indeed, an express or implied agreement to be bound by the outcome of an action will generally be enforced.[252] But it is readily apparent that the forty-one plaintiffs here never did have their due process rights respected: one roll of the dice should not bind all other players, for a judicial determination is not a gambling opportunity.

Due process of law entails ''traditional notions of fair play and substantial justice''[253] and requires that procedural sanctions imposed by courts be ''just.''[254] Due process of law requires that any deprivation of life, liberty, or property be preceded by a full and fair opportunity to be heard and to litigate. The U.S. Supreme Court in Blonder-Tongue Laboratories, Inc. v. University of Illinois Foundation[255] solemnized that ''some litigants, those who never appeared in a prior action, may not be collaterally estopped without litigating the issue. They have never had a chance to present their evidence and arguments on the claim. Due process prohibits estopping them despite one or more existing adjudications of the identical issue which stands squarely against their position.''[256]

Due process protection rests upon the existence of an interest in life, liberty, or property that the non-party possesses. The U.S. Supreme Court in 1982 in Logan v. Zimmerman Brush Co.[257] held that a cause of action is ''a species of property protected by the Fourteenth Amendment's Due Process Clause.'' But these interests to be protected can be lost, for due process limitations on personal jurisdiction can be intentionally waived;[258] the person asserting those rights can be precluded under res judicata or collateral estoppel;[259] and the due process rights can be lost through express or implied consent, as reaffirmed by the U.S. Supreme Court in 1982 in the Insurance Corporation of Ireland, Ltd. case.[260] The preclusion requisites of res judicata and collateral estoppel may be explained in the rationale that, when a non-party substantially participated in the control of the presentation of the prior suit, he should be bound thereby, as more particularly stated in Section 39 of Restatement (Second) of Judgments:

> To have control of litigation requires that a person have effective choice as to the legal theories and proofs to be advanced in behalf of the party to the action. He must also have control over the opportunity to obtain review. . . . Whether his involvement in the action is extensive enough to constitute control is a question of fact, to be resolved with reference to these criteria. It is sufficient that the choices were in the hands of counsel responsible to the controlling person; moreover, the requisite opportunity may exist even when it is shared with other persons. It is not sufficient, however, that the person merely contributed funds or advice in support of the party, supplied counsel to the party, or appeared as amicus curiae.

In the Montana case[261] the United States government was deemed to have a sufficient ''laboring oar'' in the litigation to be precluded by its results.[262] Indeed, due process requirements are met when a party voluntarily enters a relationship that allows him, as an incident to laws governing that relationship, to be precluded by the litigation of others.[263] Implied consent is the flexible and expansive justification for preclusion in an infinite number of situations.[264] But, as the highest court explained in the Logan case[265] in 1982, "[I]t has become a truism that some form of hearing is required before the owner is finally deprived of a protected property interest." Translated into words of action, this reservation delineates the requisite of an opportunity for meaningful participation in an adversary proceeding on the merits of one's claim. In 1914 the highest court demonstrated that "the fundamental requisite of due process is the opportunity to be heard,"[266] i.e., notice of the claim and personal jurisdiction over the non-party in the second action, and it is clear that such a hearing cannot be limited solely to the issue of preclusion but must constitute an opportunity for a hearing on the merits.

Preclusion of a non-party is often fostered by a recognition that the suits involve a common incident or transaction and a common opponent, as illustrated by In Re Air Crash Disaster Near Dayton, Ohio.[267] All twenty-six persons aboard a TWA jet and a private airplane that collided in mid-air were killed, and one representative of one victim successfully obtained a verdict against TWA only. On the basis of that verdict the private plane owner moved to preclude the administrator of another victim from maintaining a separate action against the private plane owner, and the trial court granted the motion to avoid repetitious litigation. The trial court opined that the prior action was prosecuted by a similarly situated litigant who adequately represented the interests of the beneficiaries of the deceased passengers' estates. But the Sixth U.S. Court of Appeals reversed, citing the following factors as grounds for reversal: (a) the second plaintiff had chosen a different attorney than the first plaintiff; (b) the second plaintiff had pursued a different trial strategy by suing the two defendants separately instead of together as the first plaintiff had done; and (c) there had been no agreement to be precluded by the result in the first case.[268] Indeed, the second plaintiff had no effective choice regarding the theories or the evidence presented, and no control over the decision not to appeal. Airplane crash cases have frequently encountered difficulties in establishing class action certification under Rule 23 of Federal Rules of Civil Procedure (FRCP) because of the tendency of the suit to degenerate into many separate lawsuits centered around "significant questions, not only of damages but of liability and defenses to liability . . . affecting individuals in different ways."[269] The opt-out provisions of Rule 23 and the disinclination of plaintiffs' attorneys to allow some other attorney to try their clients' cases[270] ensure that individual suits will be brought. However, aircraft disaster cases filed in the federal courts can be consolidated under 28 USC 1407, and even transferred to the district in which the accident took place.[271] But "mass disaster" is still one type of common incident case in which non-party preclusion is frequent and therefore repetitive litigation is precluded. In sharp contrast to the airplane disaster is the catastrophe where a large number of persons are adversely affected but the individual damages are too small to warrant individual suits, much less raise the question of non-party preclusison; in such situations, the class action is appropriate, as for civil rights violations, securities fraud scandals, and antitrust law violations.[272] In the class action context there is less reason to bind class members to issues or facts not litigated by their representatives than to issues or facts actually litigated because the element of fault in failing to raise all appropriate claims should not be imputed to nonrepresentative class members.[273]

There are a number of relatively well established exceptions to the general rule that non-parties may not be precluded by res judicata or collateral estoppel, although most of these exceptions are articulated in terms of "privity" between the precluded non-member and the party to the earlier litigation.[274] The Restatement (Second) of Judgments categorizes non-parties bound by earlier litigation in terms of their specific relationships to the parties in the earlier litigation.[275] A listing of the broad categories of persons who conventionally may be bound by the litigation of another person or persons might include (a) successors in interest, i.e., such persons obtain no more than the rights possessed by the transferor at the time of the transfer and are subject to any diminution of rights previously adjudicated against the predecessor or transferor in interest;[276] (b) owners of derivative claims, like beneficiaries suing under a wrongful death statute,[277] may be wholly precluded; (c) indemnitors or persons under obligation to indemnify may be bound under certain circumstances by the adjudication of issues adversely to the indemnitee;[278] (d) persons controlling the litigation;[279] (e) persons represented by one selected by adjudication, such as an appointed administrator or trustee or receiver, may be precluded;[280] and (f) persons precluded by agreement between the parties.[281] But the Sixth U.S. Court of Appeals in the 1981 case of Vulcan, Inc. v. Forder Cooperative[282] insisted that "federal courts are no longer bound by rigid definitions of the parties or their privies for the purpose of applying Res Judicata or Collateral Estoppel."

Citizens' expectations that a person will or will not be precluded are another aspect of the due process limitations on the application of res judicata and collateral estoppel, as perhaps illustrated by Chase National Bank v. City of Norwalk,[283] where the U.S. Supreme Court in a 1934 opinion by Justice Louis D. Brandeis rejected an argument that a non-party should be bound because he could have intervened in the prior action: "The law does not impose upon any person absolutely entitled to a hearing the burden of voluntary intervention in a suit to which he is a stranger. . . . Unless duly summoned to appear in a legal proceeding, a person not a privy may rest assured that a judgment recovered therein will not affect his legal rights." In 1980 the highest court in World-Wide Volkswagen Corp. v. Woodson[284] discussed the role of foreseeability of determining due process limitations on the assertion of personal jurisdiction; due process should permit potential parties to structure their conduct with some minimum assurance as to when and where their rights will be determined.[285] The case of Armstrong v. Manzo[286] demonstrates the evil inherent in rash preclusion; here adoption proceedings in Texas were completed without notice to the child's true father, who alleged that he had not failed to contribute adequately to the child's support and that he had received no notice of the adoption proceedings. The federal district court in Texas denied the motion to set aside the adoption decree and held that granting the father the opportunity to move to vacate satisfied any due process requisite. Fortunately, the U.S. Supreme Court reversed, pointing out that the original failure to give him notice "violated the most rudimentary demands of due process," and ordered a trial de novo.[287] Indeed, non-party preclusion penalizes a person whom the parties to the action did not join and who received no notice of the action. In Eisen v. Carlisle and Jacqueline[288] the highest court in 1974 held that the "prohibitively high cost" of providing individual notices to 2.25 million members of the class was not a valid reason for dispensing with the requisite notice in a class action. Justice Felix Frankfurter in 1951 wrote: "No better instrument has been devised for arriving at truth than to give a person in jeopardy of serious loss, notice of the case against him and the opportunity to meet it. Nor has a better way been found for generating the feeling so important to a popular government, that justice has been done."[289]

Compulsory intervention and mandatory joinder have been proposed as solutions to some of the problems of non-party preclusion, particularly the situation set forth in the Penn-Central Merger & Northwest Inclusion Cases.[290] Here the petitioner had instituted proceedings in New York to challenge the Interstate Commerce Commission's approval of a railroad merger; after the New York proceedings had been completed petitioner instituted an action in Pennsylvania. The U.S. Supreme Court ruled that the New York decision precluded further judicial review or adjudication of the same issues: "All parties with standing to challenge the Commission's action might have joined in the New York proceedings." Compulsory joinder would have made the non-parties actual parties to the lawsuit; mandatory intervention would have precluded non-parties receiving notice, whether they intervened as parties or not.[291] Judicial efficiency is probably promoted by these two proposals of compulsory joinder or mandatory intervention;[292] but forcing parties into litigation is not always the summum bonum of judicial administration.

Part and parcel of non-party preclusion is the occasional indiscriminate federal abdication to state court processes.[293] It is said that comity makes federal courts defer to state courts in limited situations; in short, federal courts "abstain," as illustrated by Tovar v. Billmeyer,[294] where the federal district court in Idaho abstained from deciding a suit brought by an applicant for a license to operate an adult book store; after a license had been denied the plaintiff filed suit in the Idaho state court, and the federal district court dismissed the suit after plaintiff lost in the state court. But the Ninth U.S. Court of Appeals reversed, holding that plaintiffs are not barred from preserving federal issues to be raised subsequently in the federal court, and the case should not have been dismissed by the federal trial court. However:

The focus . . . is upon whether exceptional circumstances exist that indicate that concurrent jurisdiction by state and federal courts is likely to cause piecemeal litigation, wasted judicial resources, inconvenience to the parties, and conflicting results. When these consequences are the likely result of concurrent jurisdiction, it is proper to consider dismissal of the federal proceeding.[295]

In Glendale Federal Savings & Loan Association v. Fox[296] the federal district court opined:

In this action, there is a possibility that the state and federal proceedings will be duplicative and that a conflict may arise between the state and federal courts. Both parties, however, have a substantial interest in having the issues presented by this action resolved. . . . Further, the issues presented are exclusively issues of federal law, and the federal court is therefore neither an inconvenient nor an inappropriate forum. . . . Given the extreme disinclination of the Supreme Court to sanction a refusal to exercise jurisdiction due to the pendency of concurrent state court litigation, this court concludes that, even without considering the presence of the Bank Board in this action, these circumstances do not justify such a refusal.

The same court in Beck v. State of California[297] echoed that

as between state and federal courts, the rule is that the pendency of an action in state court is no bar to proceedings concerning the same matter in the federal court having jurisdiction. While there are circumstances which permit the dismissal of a federal suit due to the presence of concurrent state proceedings, the circumstances are exceptional.

But a federal district court in Minnesota ruled that res judicata barred the federal suit after the Minnesota Supreme Court had found that plaintiff's First Amendment rights had not been violated when the state denied him a license to practice law: "In light of the thorough review by the Minnesota Supreme Court, it is reasonable to presume that the state court would have recognized a procedural or substantive due process violation in the denial of the petition for reinstatement. The finding that there was no denial of substantive or procedural due process inheres in the state court's opinion."[298] But a resident of Chicago did not have to file an Illinois state court suit in lieu of or prior to filing a federal court action against Chicago police for illegal search and seizure, according to the U.S. Supreme Court in Monroe v. Pape;[299] the mere availability of state judicial remedies is no bar to pursuing federal remedies. Obviously, preclusion under res judicata or collateral estoppel depends, in part, therefore, upon the resolution of jurisdiction between federal and state judicial bodies.

7

Other Forms of Preclusion

Moot cases, or cases where the controversy that originally existed between the parties before adjudication is no longer, do not fall within the jurisdiction of any court. But where the U.S. Supreme Court dismisses the moot case, leaving the lower court judgment undisturbed, collateral estoppel may preclude litigation of those issues or facts by the same parties in a subsequent suit. However, if the highest court vacates the lower court judgment in view of the mootness of the case, such judicial act nullifies the preclusive effect of that judgment.[300] Frequently, the highest court in a moot case permits the state to determine the collateral estoppel effect by remanding the moot case to the state court for proceedings, if any, deemed appropriate by the state court.[301] If the moot case arose from the federal court system, the moot case is generally vacated and remanded to the lower federal court with instructions to dismiss, as delineated in United States v. Munsingwear.[302] According to the U.S. Supreme Court, "[T]he established practice of the Court in dealing with a civil case from a court in the federal system which has become moot while on its way here or pending our decision on the merits is to reverse or vacate the judgment below and remand with a direction to dismiss."[303] This practice preserves the petitioner's chance to relitigate issues and facts, for the practice has no collateral estoppel effect. However, in pragmatic terms, the highest court's decision carries great weight as a matter of stare decisis.[304] In 1978, more than twenty-eight years after Munsingwear, the highest court in Velsicol Chemical Corp. v. United States[305] denied certiorari after the federal court of appeals had decided against Velsicol, which corporation had requested that the Court preclude collateral estoppel effect of the unreviewed judgment of the federal court of appeals. The United States government opposed Velsicol's petition because granting certiorari would vacate the judgment; the United States government was willing, however, to have the highest court decide whether it would have granted the petition for certiorari had the case not been mooted. The next year in Local 102 I.L.G.W. Union v. United States[306] the Court denied the certiorari petitions and left the lower court's decision intact again. The net effect has been a taxing of judicial resources because the litigants are permitted to bring a claim in a second suit that could have been more conveniently adjudicated in the first suit. Thus, the parties are not estopped or precluded if mootness denies them any stage of appellate review of an unfavorable judgment.

The doctrine of federal preemption originated with the Supremacy Clause of Article VI of the U.S. Constitution, and the primacy of the federal courts in determining questions of federal law and questions of fact as to which federal law is applicable has served to preclude litigants from relitigating, as evidenced by Roysdon v. R. J. Reynolds Tobacco Co.[307] Here plaintiff sued in the state court in Tennessee a cigarette manufacturer, claiming that his lung disease was the proximate result of defendant's failure to warn effectively about smoking and lung disease. The trial court directed a verdict on the defectiveness of the product at the close of plaintiff's proof but dismissed the warning claims before trial. The defendant argued that it had complied with the Cigarette Labeling and Advertising Act,[308] which provided, inter alia, that "no requirement or prohibition shall be imposed under state law with respect to advertising or promotion" of cigarettes whose packages comply with the federal statute. The federal district court found that the tort action in the state was preempted: "Exposing a manufacturer to potential damages in regards to its labeling . . . would permit a state to achieve indirectly through exposure to tort liability, what it could not directly achieve through legislation."[309] Thus, the court's imposition of duty "beyond the congressionally mandated labeling" would "thwart the stated intent of Congress to have uniformity in the warnings." In essence, preclusion under res judicata or collateral estoppel is overridden if the principle would preclude a federal court, as a consequence of a prior state court judgment, from adjudicating a claim, defense, facts, or issues implicating federal law. On the other hand, it should be noted that a federal court must, in the absence of controlling state law precedent, attempt to apply state law and interpret it as would a court of the forum state. In Jackson v. Johns-Manville Sales Corp.[310] the Fifth U.S. Court of Appeals held that under the doctrine of Erie Railroad Co. v. Tompkins[311] the federal court even in 1986 was required to interpret the law as would a Mississippi state court, although recognition must be accorded "in the absence of legislation" to the federal court's duty "to fashion federal common law in cases raising issues of uniquely federal concern," as shown in the U.S. Supreme Court 's 1981 decision in Northwest Airlines, Inc. v. Transport Workers Union.[312] However, the silence of Congress "in the face of a desperate need for federal legislation in the field of asbestos litigation does not authorize the federal judiciary to assume for itself the responsibility for formulating what essentially are legislative solutions."

Even when federal law applies to a case, a federal court may adopt state law as the federal common law if the state can be given effect without conflicting with federal policy.[313] In Montana v. United States[314] a private contractor brought suit in state court alleging the federal unconstitutionality of a state taxing statute, and the state's highest court held against the plaintiff on all constitutional questions. The U.S. Supreme Court held that ''considerations of comity as well as repose militate against redetermination of issues in a federal forum.''[315] Indeed, reversal of the highest state court determination would have thoroughly discredited the judgment of the state, and the federal court was reluctant to depart upon such unchartered waters. In essence, the preclusion of res judicata was given total effect.[316]

The civil rights statute, 42 USC 1983, was involved in McCurry v. Allen,[317] where plaintiff in a federal court action sought damages from several state police officers who allegedly violated his constitutional rights including his Fourth Amendment right to be free from illegal searches and seizures. Plaintiff had been unsuccessful in the state court. The federal district court granted the defendant's motion for summary judgment on the ground that full litigation of the issue in state court collaterally estopped plaintiff from using Section 1983 to relitigate in federal court the constitutionality of the search and seizure. The Eighth U.S. Court of Appeals reversed and held that no collateral estoppel would apply to bar that constitutional issue. But the U.S. Supreme Court deemed the holding of the Court of Appeals to be erroneous, for the doctrine of collateral estoppel is applicable to the Section 1983 suit. There is nothing in the language or legislative history of Section 1983 that discloses any congressional intent to deny binding effect to a state court judgment or decision when that state court, acting within its proper jurisdiction, has given the parties a full and fair opportunity to litigate federal claims and thereby has shown itself willing and able to protect federal rights, according to the highest court.[318] Justice Potter Stewart observed that

> the federal courts have traditionally adhered to the related doctrines of Res Judicata and Collateral Estoppel. Under Res Judicata, a final judgment on the merits of an action precludes the parties or their privies from relitigating issues that were or could have been raised in that action. . . . Under Collateral Estoppel, once a court has decided an issue of fact or law necessary to its judgment, that decision may preclude relitigation of the issue in a suit on a different cause of action involving a party to the first case. . . . As this Court and other courts have often recognized, Res Judicata and Collateral Estoppel relieve parties of the cost and vexation of multiple lawsuits, conserve judicial resources, and, by preventing inconsistent decisions, encourage reliance on adjudication. . . . In recent years, this Court has reaffirmed the benefits of Collateral Estoppel in particular, finding the policies underlying it to apply in contexts not formerly recognized at common law.[319]

Mr. Justice Stewart continued:

> The federal courts generally have also consistently accorded preclusive effect to issues decided by state courts. . . . Thus, Res Judicata and Collateral Estoppel not only reduce unnecessary litigation and foster reliance on adjudication, but also promote the comity between state and federal courts that has been recognized as a bulwark of the federal system.

Specifically, the highest court pointed to 28 USC 1738: "Judicial proceedings of any court of any state shall have the same full faith and credit in every court within the United States and its Territories and Possessions as they have by law or usage in the courts of such state . . . "; thus, Congress "has specifically required all federal courts to give preclusive effect to state court judgments whenever the courts of the state from which the judgments emerged would do so."[320] The Court then responded to the federal appellate court's concern about "a generally framed principle that every person asserting a federal right is entitled to one unencumbered opportunity to litigate that right in a federal district court, regardless of the legal posture in which the federal claim arises,"[321] in these words: "But the authority for this principle is difficult to discern. It cannot lie in the Constitution, which makes no such guarantee, but leaves the scope of the jurisdiction of the federal district court to the wisdom of Congress. And no such authority is to be found in Section 1983 itself."[322]

Where the law and/or policy has changed, frequently without any procedural protections of any kind for the affected parties, as with agency rule-making, for example, the preclusive elements of res judicata or collateral estoppel may have a decisive role to play. In the first place, when an agency changes the law or policy, courts should require a reasoned explanation of the change so that capricious changes from consistent policies or laws may be minimized.[323] But once the agency has acted, its conduct is up for judicial scrutiny, and preclusion should readily result where justified under the facts or circumstances of the case. In United States v. Georgia-Pacific Co.[324] the Ninth U.S. Court of Appeals remarked:

> Mr. Justice Holmes once wrote, "Men must turn square corners when they deal with the Government," but it is clear that the Government is itself becoming more reasonable by permitting those corners to be rounded when reason and logic demand that the Government be held to the same standard of rectilinear rectitude that it demands of its citizens. . . . We find that the dictates of both morals and justice indicate that the Government is not entitled immunity from equitable estoppel in this case.[325]

In Moser v. United States[326] the U.S. Supreme Court remarked that there was

> no need to evaluate these circumstances on the basis of any estoppel of the Government or the power of the Swiss Legation to bind the United States by its advice to petitioner. . . . because of the misleading circumstances of this case, he never had an opportunity to make an intelligent election between diametrically opposed courses required as a matter of strict law.

7.1 STARE DECISIS

Another form of preclusion, although somewhat anomalous, is the doctrine of stare decisis, which frequently mandates the dismissal of the lawsuit. But in Piccirelli v. Johns-Manville Sales Corp.[327] the New York Supreme Court, Kings County, in 1985 did not adhere to that preclusive device, and permitted a former shipyard worker to maintain his action for damages arising from his exposure to asbestos, because the court anticipated that the New York legislature would liberalize the statute of limitations (which it did in mid-1986). Plaintiff's suit was filed more than three years after his first "contact or inhalation of asbestos" and therefore was barred by Section 214 of the New York Civil Practice Law and Rules (CPLR). The court opined that it need not adhere to the preclusive doctrine of stare decisis: "This court holds that it is unreasonable to expect a person to seek his 'day in court' at a time when he cannot conceive of the fact that he might be injured." In support of its view the court asserted that the 1979 decision of the New York Court of Appeals in Matter of Higsby v. Mahoney[328] contained "a treasure chest of statements to support the proposition that 'stare decisis' does not always have to be followed." But that 1979 case did not address the duty of a court to follow controlling precedents of a higher court but only the narrow issue of whether the highest state court should overrule its earlier decision. The 1961 New York Court of Appeals decision in Greenberg v. Lorenz[329] did explain when a lower court may depart from old precedents and not give sanction to the preclusive effect of stare decisis:

> Though it is not within the competence of an intermediate appellate court to disregard controlling precedent, nevertheless, when the higher appellate courts—breaking new ground—establish a new trend, and render it clear that if the instant question were before them, they would override earlier pronouncements, it becomes the right, nay the duty, of an intermediate court, to take cognizance of it. It is then not creating one but broadening or extending the trend already set in motion by superior authority. Legal doctrines, as first enunciated, often prove to be inadequate under the impact of ensuing experience in their practical application. And when a lower court perceives a pronounced new doctrinal trend . . . it is its duty, cautiously to be sure, to follow not to resist it.

Stare decisis (which literally means "to adhere to the decided case") is based upon the notion that, when facts of two cases are essentially similar, the same rule of law should be applied to both cases. This doctrine rests firmly in the jurisprudence of justice and fairness that all persons should be treated equally before the law. The preclusive doctrine of stare decisis is also supported by the pragmatic need for certainty and constancy in the law.[330] However, it should be observed that lower courts are bound by decisions of the higher court not under the doctrine of stare decisis but by the rule of administrative convenience, which rule reflects the "pecking" order in a judicial hierarchy.[331]

To be more precise, stare decisis is shorthand for *stare decisis et non quieta movere* or "stand by past decisions and do not disturb settled things."[332] And stare decisis recognizes that a given case is a binding decision on future, similar cases; that it is the decision, not the opinion of the court, that sets the precedent which in turn is generally, not absolutely binding for future, similar cases.[333] Precedent, an integral part of the doctrine of stare decisis, is generally regarded as providing guidance in the common law.[334] But there are accepted techniques for overlooking prior decisions which establish precedent under stare decisis such as (a) denial that the prior case controls the present case; (b) distinguishment of the prior case from the present case; and (c) declaration that the prior case was "wrong."[335] Mr. Justice Frankfurter in the U.S. Supreme Court decision of Helvering v. Hallock[336] in 1940 wrote: "Stare Decisis is a principle of policy and not a mechanical formula of adherence to the latest decision, however recent and questionable, when such adherence involves collision with a prior doctrine more embracing in its scope, intrinsically sounder, and verified by experience." And Blackstone, Commentaries, long ago proclaimed:

> It is an established rule to abide by former precedents, where the same points come again in litigation. . . . Yet this rule admits of exception, where the former determination is most evidently contrary to reason; much more if it be contrary to the divine law. . . . The doctrine of the law then is this: that precedents and rules must be followed, unless flatly absurd or unjust; for though their reason be not obvious at first view, yet we owe such a deference to former times as not to suppose they acted wholly without consideration.[337]

Stare decisis requires both (a) stability and (b) flexibility, consonant with the goals of efficiency, predictability, and uniformity.[338] Indeed, "the labor of judges would be increased almost to the breaking point if every past decision could be reopened in every case and one could not lay one's own course of bricks on the very secure foundation of the courses laid by others who had gone before him," in the words of Justice Benjamin N. Cardozo more than sixty-five years ago.[339] A typical example might be the 1971 decision of the New York Court of Appeals in In Re Estate of Cairo,[340] followed in 1976 by the same court's decision in In Re Estate of Eckart.[341] In the earlier Cairo case a negative bequest in a will was deemed to be a disinheritance which barred the grandson from sharing in any property passing by intestacy; therefore, since the grandson could not benefit from any successful contest, he was held to have no standing to challenge the charitable bequest. In the later Eckart case the will stated that, if children survived the testatrix, the children should each receive a legacy of $50 and no more whatsoever; the residue of the estate was bequeathed to a charitable institution, and the children contested the bequest. Under New York law the children may contest a charitable disposition only if they were to "receive a pecuniary benefit from a successful contest."[342] The New York Appellate Division refused to follow the precedent of the Cairo case,[343] believing that the earlier decision was wrongly decided since it looked to the testatrix's intention when, under the statute, such intention was immaterial. The New York Court of Appeals, however, followed the decision in the Cairo case, holding that the nominal bequests were the functional equivalent of the disinheritance provision of the will in the Cairo case, thus rendering the precedent directly on point.[344] Indeed, strict adherence to precedents in cases involving land titles, commercial transactions, and contracts should apply with equal force to the law governing wills. In declining to upset the settled precedent the highest New York court deferred to the principle that the legislature is capable of changing a statue if necessary and desirable, but in the interim, courts should abide by the preclusive doctrine of stare decisis.

Another requisite of stare decisis is flexibility, which may involve both implied overruling and anticipatory overruling, the former occurring when the higher court, without mentioning that it is overturning its previous decision, determines that the rule of law that the precedent enunciated is no longer correct,[345] and the latter occurring when a lower court departs from a higher court's decision embodying a rule of law that the higher court has not repudiated either explicitly or by implication.[346] (It is interesting to note that both England and Israel have strictly construed stare decisis and leave little room for flexibility.)[347] Implied overruling is not a troublesome situation, for such departure from precedent is based upon an almost normal, judicial bureaucratic action; but anticipatory overruling is a departure from that normal, judicial bureaucratic action, as the lower court gives flexibility to the precedent, as delineated in Rowe v. Payton,[348] where the Fourth U.S. Court of Appeals stated: "This court, of course, must follow the Supreme Court, but there are occasional situations in which subsequent Supreme Court opinions have so eroded an older case, without explicitly overruling it, as to warrant a subordinate court in pursuing what it conceives to be a clearly defined new lead from the Supreme Court to a conclusion inconsistent with an older Supreme Court case."[349] Mr. Justice Cardozo in his monumental treatise "The Nature of the Judicial Process" in 1921 expounded: "There should be a greater readiness to abandon an untenable position when the rule to be discarded may not reasonably be supposed to have determined the conduct of the litigants, and particularly when in its origin it was the product of institutions or conditions which have gained a new significance or development with the progress of the years."[350] One example of such reexamination in the realm of tort law was the development of strict liability in products liability litigation.[351] Still another example is found in Silver v. Great American Insurance Co.,[352] which reexamined in 1972 the prior New York rule that forum non conveniens would not be invoked if one of the parties was a New York resident. The New York Court of Appeals determined that reason and justice required relaxation of this rule and that residency should be only one of several factors, especially in view of the great mobility of populations.[353] And in People v. Hobson[354] the highest New York court observed that the relative recency of a case does not determine that it should be accorded stare decisis effect:

> Stare Decision, if it is to be more than shibboleth, requires more subtle analysis. Indeed, the true doctrine by its own vitality should not, perversely, give to its violation strength and stability. That would be like the parricide receiving mercy because he is now an orphan. The odd case rode roughshod over Stare Decisis and now would be accorded Stare Decisis as their legitimate right, whether or not they express sound, good, or acceptable doctrine.[355]

It might be observed that even an *obiter dicta* can alter a precedent and thereby give stability and flexibility to stare decisis, as illustrated by the U.S. Supreme Court's 1966 adoption in A Book Named "John Cleland's Memoirs of a Woman of Pleasure" v. Attorney General of Massachusetts,[356] which case set forth the test of "utterly without redeeming social value" as the definition of obscenity; clearly, the test was derived from an obscure dicta in the 1957 decision of the same court in Roth v. United States.[357]

An arbitration award on a particular material issue may be deemed to be stare decisis and may have a binding effect in a subsequent lawsuit, according to the New York Appellate Division, Third Dept., in Clemens v. Apple.[358] Here plaintiff, a victim of Alzheimer's disease, was involved in an automobile accident, and sued the defendant for aggravation of his disc condition. But in a prior arbitration proceeding against his insurer the plaintiff had lost the very claim based upon the lack of a causal connection between the automobile accident and the disc condition. Defendant herein successfully argued that plaintiff was now collaterally estopped to sue defendant for the same physical injury which was not caused by the automobile accident. Thus, the arbitrator's earlier decision was given stare decisis effect.

8

Insurance Policies and the Preclusive Devices of Waiver, Estoppel, and Election

The principles of waiver and estoppel are active throughout the law, but these devices are especially significant (along with the device of election) in the law of insurance,[359] due to two circumstances: (1) the harsh and outworn doctrine of warranty had worked intolerable hardships upon the insureds; and (2) the ancient theory of the common law that a party to a written contract must be held to know and assent to all the terms of the contract, despite the fact that the insurance contract is one of adhesion and the insured had little recourse.[360] The preclusive devices of waiver, estoppel, and election were created as corrective tools. Waiver is defined as the intentional relinquishment of a known right, but it also includes the intended giving up of a known privilege or power; waiver may be express or implied from circumstances, but it always involves consent, express or implied. Estoppel arises when the insurer or the insured has brought about or permitted such conditions as make it inequitable for the insured or the insurer to claim a right to which the insured or insurer would otherwise be entitled; if either the insured or the insurer makes, by word or act, a false representation of fact with reference to the contract upon which the other, acting in good faith, reasonably relies to his prejudice, he will not be allowed to make any claim under the terms of the insurance policy which is inconsistent with such representation. Election is generally delineated as a manifested choice by the insured or the insurer having the power to choose or elect definitively one of two alternative legal relations and having knowledge of the facts which gave him or it such power. Thus, waiver and election rest on contractual agreement, while estoppel is tortious, grounded on deceit or at least upon conduct that is misleading; waiver and election give effect to the intention of the party waiving or electing, while an estoppel is enforced by the court to defeat the inequitable intent of the party estopped.

The above distinctions between waiver, estoppel, and election are not always respected by the courts. The U.S. Supreme Court in 1877 asserted that "the doctrine of waiver, as asserted, against insurance companies to avoid the strict enforcement of conditions contained in their policies, is only another name for the doctrine of estoppel."[361] A federal district court in Iowa in 1956 spoke with this technical understanding:

> The conduct of the plaintiff could not be considered to work an Estoppel because there was no evidence of a representation or holding out by the plaintiff or of reliance by the defendant. Neither can the conduct of the plaintiff be considered to operate as a Waiver strictly speaking, because the plaintiff never manifested to the defendant that it intended to relinquish its right to assert the condition. However, the conclusion seems inescapable that its conduct did constitute an Election to treat the policy as being in effect as to coverage of the defendant."[362]

Indeed, waiver is sometimes broadly used to indicate merely the legal consequence that a particular defense by the insurer is not available to the insurer because of some conduct of the insurer or its agents. Estoppel always involves the notion of reliance by the insured upon the conduct of the insurer, but varies in meaning with the kind of conduct of the insurer which may give rise to a representation of fact (estoppel by misrepresentation), or a promise (promissory estoppel). Election is clearly a manifest choice or election by the person having the power to do so, a unilateral undertaking.

Waiver litigation frequently highlights at least three aspects of the insured's conduct, to wit: (1) the importance or relative unimportance of the deviation in conduct or defect in the policy; courts will more readily find waiver of an immaterial breach of warranty than permit waiver to extend the scope of the insured event; (2) the scope of the actual or apparent authority of the agent whose conduct is the basis of the waiver; waivers by the home office of the insurer are more apt to be respected; and (3) the extent of the insured's change of position in reliance on the conduct of the insurer. In Phoenix Insurance Co. v. Ross Jewelers, Inc.[363] burglars had broken into a retail jewelry store and made away with valuable merchandise. Although the vault had a protective alarm system, it was the store manager's habit to leave the key in the lock; this fact as well as the insured's failure to keep "a detailed and itemized inventory" were known to the insurer. The Fifth U.S. Court of Appeals affirmed a holding that there was a waiver: "While it may be said that waiver depends upon intention, the intention may be inferred from acts and conduct. Such inference is fully warranted under the facts established here." On the other hand, the Michigan Supreme Court in Ruddock v. Detroit Life Insurance Co.[364] found no waiver; here the insured had died in the military service and the policy expressly excluded such coverage, although the insurer had advised the plaintiff beneficiary to have an administrator appointed to collect the proceeds of the policy. In essence, the court simply refused to broaden or extend the coverage of the policy; furthermore, the insurer had no knowledge at the time that the insured had died in the military service, so that the insurer could not have waived that unknown fact. In Atlas Assurance Co. v. Standard Brick & Tile Corp.[365] there was an unwatched brick plant, i.e., the insured failed to comply with the watchman's clause in the fire policies; but the court found no waiver on the part of the insurer even though the insurer had knowledge of the unwatched brick plant: "Even though we indulge in the dubious assumption that the plaintiff-insurers were familiar with the character of watchman's service maintained by the defendant-insured, they were under no obligation to cancel or void the policies, and their failure in this respect, standing alone, would not constitute waiver." In John Hancock Mutual Life Insurance Co. v. Luzio[366] the Ohio Supreme Court found no waiver on the part of the insurer; here an agent, probably in collusion with the insured, issued an industrial policy on the life of the decedent, who had tuberculosis, a fact which if known to the insurer would have precluded issuance of the policy. The court observed willful concealment on the part of the insured, and emphasized that the agent had no authority to waive a material misstatement, especially since the industrial policy then did not require a physical examination before issuance of the policy. In contrast thereto is the situation where "the company by its act lulls the vigilance of the insured into inactivity so far as furnishing proof of loss is concerned. . . . The evidence amply warranted a finding that the defendant-insurer by its conduct waived the filing of a formal proof of loss within the 60-day period."[367]

Estoppel is illustrated by Welch v. Fire Association of Philadelphia,[368] where the Wisconsin Supreme Court found an estoppel by representation of law; the insurer defended upon the ground that the insured building destroyed in the fire had been on leased ground in violation of the policy:

> If an insurance company delivers one of its policies and receives the premium therefor with knowledge of the facts rendering it void when its terms are applied to such facts, in legal effect it thereby assures its customer that, as regards the contract, the condition of the property shall be considered in all respects according to the calls of the contract, regardless of the truth of the matter, and invites him to rely thereon; and such invitation being accepted, the company is ESTOPPED from thereafter changing its position to the prejudice of the assured, though the policy declares that no condition thereof is subject to waiver except by written agreement indorsed thereon or added thereto. . . .

Sixty-six years later in Madgett v. Monroe County Mutual Tornado Insurance Co.[369] the same court viewed a different situation, to wit: plaintiff bought a farm and took possession on the first of the month; the vendor had an unexpired windstorm policy on the farm. When a windstorm thirteen days later damaged the buildings on the farm, the plaintiff made a list of the damages and presented it to a director of the defendant insurance company, but later the company declined to pay. The court opined:

> Estoppel is a sturdy doctrine, but it cannot sustain so heavy a load. Estoppel can block, but it cannot create. It is a barricade. . . . It is not a bulldozer. . . . Estoppel may prevent an insurer from enforcing certain policy provisions against its insured. However, even where the relationship of insurer and insured exists, estoppel cannot be used to enlarge the coverage of an insurance policy, for then the effect would be to create . . . a new contract providing coverage for which no premium has been paid.

In Mentz v. Lancaster Fire Insurance Co.[370] an agent for a fire insurance company issued additional insurance in another insurer to the plaintiff; the first policy with defendant insurer expressly declared void the contract if additional insurance on the same property was procured without the defendant insurer's written permission. The agent had given the insured assurance that the coverages were proper. The Pennsylvania Supreme Court ruled that the defendant insurer was estopped to deny liability since the insured had relied upon the agent's assurances of proper coverages; furthermore, the insured could not read English, and was lulled into security by the agent's assurances. But a general local agent cannot bind the insurer by assent outside the scope of his authority, as illustrated by Blair v. National Reserve Insurance Co.[371] Here the furniture in a given house was moved without the assent of the insurer, although the general local agent in a telephone conversation with the insured had assented to the removal of the insured furniture: "Authority to make the original contract or to waive the condition in the manner prescribed therein is not enough. . . . Some further and additional delegation of authority derived from the fountain head of corporate power must be shown broad enough to include the abrogation of the condition in a manner excluded by the very terms of the contract itself."[372] Yet the Arkansas Supreme Court in Sovereign Camp v. Richardson[373] ruled that the insurer was estopped from denying the local agent's promissory representation that the military exclusion clause in the policy would not be enforced as members of the mutual benefit society were being enrolled as beneficiaries of the policy. According to the court, the insurer must be estopped, "for [not] to do so would enable it to take advantage of its own wrong and perpetrate a fraud."

An insured represented to his insurer that the collision giving rise to a claim against him was not due either to his intoxication or to his negligence; on the strength of these assurances the insurer declined offers of settlement up to the policy limits. But the jury was unpersuaded by the insured's defenses and returned a heavy verdict against the insured over and above the policy limits. The insured then sued the insurer for bad faith in refusing to settle within the policy limits, and the insurer countered with the argument that the insured was estopped from making that claim of bad faith. The Seventh U.S. Court of Appeals affirmed a lower court ruling disallowing the estoppel against the insured: "Under some circumstances, in order to act in good faith, an insurer may be required to disbelieve its insured."[374] In Watson v. U.S. Fidelity & Guaranty Co.[375] the Ninth U.S. Court of Appeals pointed out that to justify an estoppel

> there must be conduct, acts, language or silence amounting to a representation or concealment of material facts. . . . Defendant [insurer] did not misrepresent the nature of the coverage under the policy. On the contrary, the policy clearly stated that coverage was limited to cars not owned by members of the family. Plaintiffs were ignorant of the true nature of the policy only because none of them read it. . . . Estoppel does not erase the duty of due care and is not available for the protection of one who has suffered loss solely by reason of his own failure to act or inquire.

The Fifth U.S. Court of Appeals in Travelers Indemnity Co. v. Holman[376] favored the policyholder and estopped the insurer from denying coverage for business pursuits. It appears that the owner of a dwelling house which produced income was apprehensive about his liability insurance coverage, but the insurer's local agent and one of its field underwriters had agreed that the coverage was adequate. When the claim arose the insurer denied liability upon the basis of an exclusion for business pursuits. But the court circumvented the defense based upon a "practical construction" of the policy of insurance, upon the fact that the insurer's own underwriter had made a classification of risks and status under the policy, and finally: "In a nutshell . . . the underwriter's commitment was a supplemental contract based on promissory estoppel, a contractual concept, not a mere instance of estoppel in pais." Indeed, the insurer's conduct may be held to raise an estoppel under such circumstances as the following: delivery of a policy with knowledge that it is voidable for breach of condition contained therein and collecting a sound premium therefor;[377] the act of the insurer's agent in misinterpreting questions in the application or in falsifying the answers thereto in such a manner as to mislead the insured into thinking that the questions are truly answered, when in fact the questions are not answered;[378] and express or implied statements that acts required by the policy to be done by the insurer such as indorsement of consent or other notation thereon, have been done, when in fact these acts have not been done.[379]

Election is a deliberate, manifested choice by the insurer having the power to choose definitively between two or more legal relationships and having that specific or special knowledge of the facts which give the insurer such power of choice.[380] In Knickerbocker Life Insurance Co. v. Norton[381] the U.S. Supreme Court observed that the insured had taken out a policy on his life and had paid the premium with $50 cash and two promissory notes due two and three months in the future. When the time of maturity of the notes was reached, the insurer's agent orally allowed extension, although the son of the insured had paid one note after maturity. The policy had expressly stated that the proceeds were forfeited if the premiums were not paid on time and that the agents cannot waive such forfeiture. But the highest court deemed that the insurer here had "elected" to condone the breach of the time payment clause by the conduct of its agent in not cancelling the policy of insurance; the court found the existence of a practice of the insurer which gave its agents authority to accept and extend the payment of such premium notes. Above all, election here satisfied the legal abhorrence of forfeitures,[382] and the insurer was effectively precluded from asserting the defense otherwise. In Madden v. Interstate Business Men's Accident Association[383] the insured had misrepresented in an application for accident insurance that in 1914 he was not deformed nor crippled; in 1915 he was injured in an accident, and five months later the insurer learned of the material misrepresentation, cancelled the policy, and returned the unearned premium. The insured contended that these acts of the insurer constituted an election that a valid insurance had existed at the time of the accident, and the Minnesota Supreme Court agreed: "If the insurer chooses, with full knowledge of the ground of forfeiture, to consider the policy in force and makes an Election accordingly, it cannot insist upon a forfeiture. It has waived it. . . . The company's conduct was a conclusive concession that the policy was in force, and that no right of forfeiture was claimed when the cancellation was made. . . ."

One of the insurer's common defenses to an action on the policy is the lack of an insurable interest on the part of the insured; in Prudential Insurance Co. v. Tutalo[384] the insurer in the 1930s followed the common practice of filing a bill of interpleader and paying the policy proceeds into court if there was a dispute as to who was entitled to the proceeds. The Rhode Island court followed the general rule that the payment of the proceeds into court constituted an election by the insurer of any defense including the lack of insurable interest. But in Bell v. National Life & Accident Insurance Co.[385] the Alabama court refused to apply election or waiver or estoppel: here the plaintiff had paid her aunt's funeral and burial expenses when the insurer's agent encouraged her to insure her uncle's life so that she would not have to pay funeral and burial expenses when her uncle died. After her uncle died there was no proof that plaintiff had any legal duty to pay his funeral expenses, i.e., she had no insurable interest in her uncle's life, so that the insurer refused to make payment. On the other hand, in Roberts v. National Benefit Life Insurance Co.,[386] a South Carolina court stated that the insurable interest requirement was waived because the insurer knew that the beneficiary had no insurable interest, even though the policy had been bought by the insured. In Light v. Countrymen's Mutual Fire Insurance Co.[387] the Pennsylvania court in 1895 ruled that the insurer had elected to overlook the defense of lack of insurable interest: here the insured had sold the insured property but had secured a judgment for the unpaid balance of the purchase price, and as an unsecured creditor would not have an insurable interest in the property which no longer belonged to him.

But an officer of the insurer new all the facts of the transaction and had advised the insured to pay the premium and keep the policy in force long after the property was sold. The court simply expounded that "to permit such a defense [of lack of insurable interest] to be made would be highly inequitable and unjust."[388] And in Republic Insurance Co. v. Silverton Elevators, Inc.[389] the Texas Supreme Court faced a situation involving a fire insurance policy issued to S covering S's house and the personal property therein; but the house was used by T, a manager and employee of S, and the personal property in the house was owned by T. Only S was named as the insured in the policy, and after a loss occurred the insurer refused to pay the claim for damages to the personal property of T because T was not an insured under the policy and S had no insurable interest in T's personal property. The district court entered judgment for the amount of the policy in favor of S "for the use and benefit" of T, and the highest Texas court affirmed: "Issuance of the policy and collection of the premiums with full knowledge of the facts operates as a waiver of any requirement that the named insured own or possess a beneficial interest in the insured property."[390]

Collateral estoppel also plays a prominent role in insurance policy litigation as illustrated by Farmers Insurance Co. of Arizona v. Vagnozzi,[391] where the Arizona Supreme Court ruled that the insurer was not collaterally estopped from raising its defense of intentionally caused injuries in a subsequent declaratory judgment action after the insured had obtained partial summary judgment in another proceeding which established the insured's negligence as a matter of law.[392] The accident occurred during a basketball game when Vagnozzi knocked down the insured, who retaliated by angrily swinging his arm at Vagnozzi's chest, causing Vagnozzi to fall backwards onto the concrete floor, hitting his head and losing consciousness. The Arizona Supreme Court, in ruling against application of collateral estoppel, created an exception to the principle that an insurer that defends an insured is collaterally estopped from contesting issues essential to the judgment in the tort action.[393] But it is self-evident here that there was a conflict of interests between the insured and the insurer, and that the insurer was not a party to the initial suit between the insured and Vagnozzi, which suit may have involved "sharp practices" that the court might have condemned.[394] It should be noted that the insurer did meet its duty to defend the insured by retaining an attorney for the insured in the initial suit. But collateral estoppel does not preclude insurers and insureds from relitigating issues as to which a conflict of interest existed in the earlier tort action. In effect, the court here adopted Section 58 of Restatement (Second) of Judgments,[395] which recognizes that a party is not precluded from contesting issues determined in an action in which it appeared in one legal capacity when it appears in a second action in a different legal capacity, and there is a conflict of interest between the two legal capacities. In its legal capacity as indemnitor the insurer is not liable for the judgment against the insured in the action in which it defended its insured, it the claim itself is outside the scope and coverage of the insurance policy.[396] An indemnitor is not collaterally estopped from contesting any issues determined in a prior suit where conflict of interest with the indemnitee or insured prevented the indemnitor or insurer from defending. But if the insurer breached its duty to defend the insured in the prior suit, the insurer would be collaterally estopped from contesting issues determined in that action in which it refused to defend the insured. Section 58 of Restatement (Second) of Judgments in Comment a explained the application of collateral estoppel to enforce the duty to defend:

> The duty to provide a defense is enforced by rules creating strong disincentives against default in performance of the duty. One such rule is that if the indemnitor fails to assume the defense of the action involving a claim that "might be found to be" within the indemnity obligation, he is precluded from contesting not only the existence and extent of the indemnitee's liability to the injured person but also the obligation to indemnify.[397]

Offensive collateral estoppel[398] has been approved in many insurance cases, such as Seguros Tepeyac, S. A. v. Jernigan,[399] where the Fifth U.S. Court of Appeals held that an automobile liability insurer was precluded from relitigating the meaning of the terms of the insurance policy where these terms, including the insurer's claim to a liability exclusion clause, were fully investigated in a prior action brought in the same federal district court in Texas by the passenger against the insurer. These policy terms were deemed essential to the judgment rendered in the prior suit against the insurer. The court rejected the insurer's argument as to the need for identity of parties. Defensive collateral estoppel was approved in Home Owners Federal Savings & Loan Association v. Northwestern Fire & Marine Insurance Co.;[400] here the plaintiff bank in an action against the insurance company was collaterally estopped from alleging that certain other fire insurance policies containing the "errors and ommissions" clause, were not in full force and effect on the day of the fire, since, in the prior action by the same plaintiff against another insurer, the plaintiff was defeated on that very issue after full and complete litigation.

Collateral estoppel has unfortunately been utilized to extend the coverage of an insurance contract, as shown in Taylor v. Commercial Union Insurance Co.,[401] where the Eighth U.S. Court of Appeals ruled against the insurer on the basis of its denial of coverage to the insured; it seems that the insured, after its insured barges damaged the property of another, had incorporated itself, and after being sued successfully by the damaged dockowner, paid the judgment in the name of the incorporated entity. The insurer then argued that the unincorporated entity was the only insured, and so the insurer had no obligation to indemnify the incorporated entity. The court observed that the insurer, after the barge damages had occurred, had contacted the attorney for the incorporated entity to inquire about the accident, and had actually encouraged the incorporated entity to defend the claim. The court held that, although the insurer could have denied recovery to an entity that it did not insure, its failure to do so and the fact that the incorporated entity relied to its detriment on a material representation made by the insurer, estopped the insurer from denying coverage.[402] This minority opinion is at variance with the great majority of court opinions that collateral estoppel may not be used to extend coverage of an insurance policy.[403]

9

Collateral Estoppel in Action

The preclusive device of collateral estoppel can perhaps best be examined as the device appears ''in action.'' Hereinafter set forth is a delineation of personal injuries and products liability (Section 9.1); medical malpractice (Section 9.2); mass accidents and class actions (Section 9.3); administrative agencies (Section 9.4); governments (Section 9.5); arbitration (Section 9.6); tax frauds (Section 9.7); and criminal conduct (Section 9.8). Yet the scope of this preclusive device truly has no parameters, as illustrated by the recent New York decision in Grinton Investments N.V. v. Estragon Realty Corp.[404] Here the defendants contracted to purchase eighteen acres of undeveloped land from a society and to assign the property to the plaintiff. The individual defendants subsequently contracted to sell the stock of the plaintiff corporation, whose sole asset was the real property in question. Plaintiff seeks the property in order to develop it for condominiums, and has expended funds in reliance on the expected purchase of the land by defendants. The closing date was extended twice by adding \$100,000 to the purchase price of \$3 million before plaintiff itself ''consummated the purchase of the real estate.'' Plaintiff now seeks a preliminary injunction against the defendants from interfering with his direct purchase of the land, and rests his motion upon equitable estoppel. The court noted that

> Estoppel is an induced rightful reliance by word or conduct that causes the relying party to alter its conduct based on this reliance to its detriment. . . . The prior course of conduct in formalizing agreement to adjourn the closing directly affects the type of words or conduct that could justifiably induce an alteration in conduct by the plaintiff. . . . This reliance must be justified, . . . and this justified reliance has not been established in this case. The plaintiff's change in conduct merely to secure a lower

interest rate for its own benefit cannot be considered reliance on the defendants' actions. The court finds that the plaintiff has failed to demonstrate a likelihood of success on the merits or a favorable balance of the equities. . . .

The real estate field is an attractive avenue for preclusive devices like collateral estoppel, for the stakes are high and the opportunities for deception are acute.

9.1 PERSONAL INJURIES AND PRODUCTS LIABILITY

The fields of personal injuries, negligence, and products liability are fertile for the utilization of the preclusive device of collateral estoppel because judicial economy may be realistically promoted, especially where the issues are straightforward, the parties are limited in numbers, and the preclusive effect can be expertly tailored to the particular circumstances. In Southern Pacific Transportation Co. v. Smith Material Corp.,[405] for example, the plaintiff railroad relied upon a prior judgment that it was 25 percent liable and the defendant truck company was 75 percent liable for the collision, and the Fifth U.S. Court of Appeals approved of plaintiff's utilization of offensive collateral estoppel to limit its liability, unless the railroad was sued by a passenger seeking to hold the railroad to a higher standard of care.[406] In McHone v. Montgomery Ward, Inc.[407] the father of a minor injured on an escalator in defendant's department store sued for the minor's medical expenses and loss of services, and was successful in establishing the liability of the department store; in the suit by minor against the same defendant for personal injuries the federal district court in Ohio authorized the minor to invoke collateral estoppel to preclude the defendant from relitigating the matter. And in Ragnar Benson, Inc. v. Jungclaus Co.[408] the plaintiff construction worker filed a personal injury action against the contractor, who in turn filed a cross-action against the subcontractor, but the cross-complaint was dismissed for failure to state a cause of action. A second plaintiff filed a companion action against the contractor arising out of the same accident, and the contractor served a cross-complaint against the subcontractor, who predicated his defense on collateral estoppel in that in the first action the court dismissed the cross-complaint for failure to state a cause of action. The Indiana appellate court agreed with the subcontractor in precluding the cross-claim by the contractor.

The preclusive effect in personal injury actions, like most other tort actions, does not necessarily have to be limited to the same cause of action. In Collins v. Seaboard Coastline Railroads Co.[409] a federal district court in Georgia authorized the wife of an injured automobile passenger to use the previous court ruling in her husband's personal injury suit to preclude defendant from relitigating liability in her action for loss of consortium. However, Alderman v. Chrysler Corp.,[410] decided by a federal district court in Virginia, adds confusion to the preclusive effect by its almost ludicrous result, to wit: the plaintiff in her individual suit for personal injuries lost the case, but, in her capacity as administratrix of the estate of her late husband, she won! According to the court, it had to balance the unfairness of allowing the plaintiff to relitigate the breach of warranty allegation against the unfairness of preclusion to beneficiaries who were not parties to the first suit. (The court overlooked the fact that the plaintiff herself was also one of the beneficiaries of her husband's estate.) And in Goodson v. McDonough Power Equipment, Inc.[411] the Ohio court refused preclusive effect to an out-of-state decision adverse to the defendant manufacturer of a lawnmower whose faulty design allegedly caused personal injuries to the plaintiff child; the court reasoned that there could be no issue preclusion in relitigation of product design issues relating to mass-produced products, particularly when the first adjudication arose out of a separate underlying incident.

Utilization of collateral estoppel in products liability actions involves both benefits and risks to the litigants.[412] The benefits are possible when a defendant has manufactured a defective or inherently dangerous product that injures many users so that the issues presented are believed to be identical, although in practice the issues seldom are identical; judicial economy as well as savings for the litigants can result here from the preclusive device. On the other hand, risks are inherent in precluding the defendant product manufacturer when the issues are not narrowly construed and the preclusive effect is too expansive. The note writer in 15 New England Law Review 1 (1979), in a footnote,[413] endeavored to balance the "prejudice quotient" with the "evidence of a significant probative thrust" in two examples: (1) in the first case, the plaintiff proves that he had a perfectly healthy arterial system before he took defendant's drug product, which allegedly causes users to sustain hardening of the arteries; plaintiff experiences a stroke after consuming the product; and (2) in the second case, the plaintiff had an arterial system that was in bad shape, took very little exercise, had a high-cholesterol diet, was overweight, and smoked cigarettes; after consuming defendant's drug product the plaintiff also experiences a stroke. If collateral estoppel were to lie in the second case, the jury would be instructed that the drug product was defective, and the second plaintiff's burden of proof as to liability would be lightened, notwithstanding that the defendant manufacturer could still argue that plaintiff's extremely poor health was the proximate cause of his stroke; the application of collateral estoppel would be greatly prejudicial to the defendant product manufacturer. The court might want to employ "a careful balancing test to see if the probative value of the estoppel on the issue of a defect is outweighed by the prejudice that may result to the defendant on the issue of causation." Citing International Shoe Machinery Corp. v. United Shoe Machinery Corp.,[414] the note writer concluded:

> Since the applicability of an estoppel is an evidentiary question (the estoppel takes the place of independent evidence on the issue it relates to), pursuant to well-established principles, it may be argued that even where there is no technical obstacle preventing its application, the trial judge should have discretionary authority to bar same, if its probative value is outweighed by its prejudicial effect.

The federal district court in Texas in 1980 in Flatt v. Johns-Manville Sales Corp.[415] permitted the plaintiff to preclude two asbestos manufacturers from relitigating several issues which were elements of the strict liability cause of action, although one manufacturer had not been involved in previous litigation and furthermore did not manufacture the type of asbestos product which had been the subject of the earlier litigation. But the plaintiff had succeeded in convincing the court that *all* products containing asbestos were defective and unreasonably dangerous to users, that asbestos was a known cause of lung diseases, and that no state-of-the-art defense should be considered in evidence.[416] The probability of inconsistent verdicts did not prohibit preclusion, according to the court; and furthermore, the defendants should have anticipated the preclusive effect. Four years later the Texas Supreme Court in Bonniwell v. Beech Aircraft Corp.[417] was faced with a situation where in the prior suit the defendant manufacturer was found not negligent nor liable for a design defect in the aircraft; the court refused to apply collateral estoppel against the plaintiffs in a subsequent suit where they appeared as assignees of the aircraft operator's claim for indemnity, although in the prior suit the operator and seller of the aircraft were found negligent. The court pointed out that the issue of comparative negligence was not essential to the prior judgment, and hence the liability of the defendant manufacturer could be relitigated. Three dissenting judges of the court argued that

> application of the doctrine of collateral estoppel is appropriate where the derivative claims of identical parties are based upon issues identical to those litigated in a prior suit. . . . The doctrine of collateral estoppel precludes relitigation of the comparative fault issue as between the same defendants . . . [who] are now barred from relitigating the issue as to who was to blame for the crash. . . . Any judgment granting or denying indemnity or contribution . . . is necessarily dependent upon adjudication of liabilities. Where defendants have established adversity by opposing each other in a cross-claim, a judgment between them establishes their rights as to each other. . . . For these reasons, it is clear that the issue of comparative fault of the parties was fully and fairly litigated.[418]

In 1984 the Utah Supreme Court affirmed a judgment that the defendant product manufacturer was liable for damages sustained by an infant allegedly resulting from her mother's ingestion of defendant's drug Delalutin during pregnancy.[419] In 1985 another infant brought suit in New York against the same drug product manufacturer alleging the same injuries, and the New York court was called upon by the new plaintiff to apply collateral estoppel.[420] But the New York court responded:

> To allow the doctrine of collateral estoppel to be used to deny a defendant in a case such as this an opportunity to introduce evidence clearly relevant to a key issue in the case, the absence or existence of a causal relationship between the claimed defect in the product produced by such defendant and used by the plaintiffs, and the injuries for

which plaintiffs are suing, is the use of that doctrine to deny such a defendant a complete and fair opportunity to litigate the very issue upon which its rights depend.[421]

The New York court pointed out that

there is reliable evidence available now, which if it had been available at the time of the Barson (1984) trial, might have led to a different verdict. . . . Specifically, the defendants can in 1985 prove that the product lacked teratogenesis, which is the origin or mode of production of a malformed fetus.

In Olivarez v. Broadway Hardware, Inc.[422] the Texas Court of Civil Appeals focused upon an action against the retailer of a pellet gun for personal injuries sustained by the plaintiff when the weapon accidentally discharged. In the subsequent suit the retailer sought to invoke collateral estoppel to preclude relitigation of his non-liability, but the court ruled that the retailer was only entitled to invoke the preclusion as to liability issues raised by plaintiffs in the previous action against the manufacturer and distributor of the pellet gun; collateral estoppel would not serve as a bar to allegations regarding the retailer's alleged failure to warn plaintiff-purchaser at the time of the sale of the pellet gun as well as other allegations not essential to the general verdict rendered in the prior suit against all other defendants.

The case of Thompson v. Continental Emsco Co.[423] presents the issue of settlement and collateral estoppel. Here the injured seaman sought enforcement of what he regarded as a binding settlement agreement, but the federal district court in Texas thought otherwise. Initially the court noted that plaintiff must prove by a preponderance of the evidence that an oral agreement was reached regarding all the material terms of the settlement agreement. The burden of proof that counsel did not have actual authority to settle the case is upon the defendant. Authority to settle must be express or the facts must be such as to result in collateral estoppel, according to the court. Here enforcement was denied because defense counsel did not believe that he had authority for the alleged settlement amount; furthermore, defendant did not authorize the settlement amount nor ratify it, according to the court.

9.2 MEDICAL MALPRACTICE

While collateral estoppel and other preclusive devices are fully applicable to the medical malpractice situation as well as other tortious acts or omissions, courts have been somewhat reluctant to benefit the defendant physician by invoking the protection of collateral estoppel. Indeed, the doctrine of collateral estoppel "may bar a defendant physician from asserting the statute of limitations as an affirmative defense to plaintiff's cause of action to recover damages for wrongful death of a decedent where there are evidentiary facts which show purposeful concealment and misrepresentation of facts and consequences of malpractice,'' according to the New York Appellate Division, Second Dept., in McIvor v. DiBenedetto.[424] Where there is ''justifiable reliance upon the defendant's intentional misrepresentation which prevented the plaintiff from discovering the malpractice or induced him or her to refrain from bringing suit,'' the New York court would invoke collateral estoppel, unless ''the plaintiff possesses 'timely knowledge' sufficient to place him or her under a duty to make inquiry and ascertain all the relevant facts prior to the expiration of the applicable statute of limitations.''[425] The New York court found that the plaintiff's admissions here ''negate, as a matter of law, an essential element of equitable estoppel, i.e., justifiable reliance upon appellant's intentional misrepresentations which prevented her from discovering the malpractice or induced her to refrain from bringing suit.'' Accordingly, the court granted the physician's motion for partial summary judgment dismissing the action insofar as it was asserted against the physician as barred by the two-year statute of limitations.

The existence of a default judgment or a confession of judgment will collaterally estop a malpractice cause of action arising from the same transaction.[426] In Kossover v. Trattler[427] the defendant physician had previously sued plaintiff to recover for professional services rendered; when the patient failed to answer the complaint, a default judgment was entered. Subsequently, plaintiff commenced an action for medical malpractice covering the same period of time, and prior to trial the defendant physician moved to amend his answer to include the affirmative defenses of collateral estoppel and res judicata, contending that the default judgment precluded the malpractice claim. But the trial court denied the motions, pointing out that collateral estoppel should not apply since plaintiff's ''absence'' in the prior action prevented the court from considering the malpractice issue. On appeal the New York Appellate Division, Second Dept., affirmed, pointing out that the lack of identical issues between the prior and subsequent actions negated the invocation of the preclusion device. However, the concurring opinion commented that ''implicit in the finding [in the first suit] that the fee was earned . . . [was] a finding that the treatment was beneficial and therefore not the proper subject for future litigation on the malpractice action by the patient.'' The holding in this New York case is consonant with Section 58 of Restatement (Second) of Judgments, which in Comment b, Illustration 3, poses the same set of facts, to wit: ''A, a physician, brings an action against B for medical services rendered to B. B fails to plead and judgment by default is given against him. B is not precluded from subsequently maintaining an action against A for malpractice and recovering for harm done to him by such malpractice.'' It is submitted that such a rule of law presents the ludicrous situation where the physician collects a fee of $100,000 for professional services rendered, yet loses the subsequent malpractice suit for $100,000, thereby effecting a ''washout'' which decided nothing! There is little reason why a patient cannot litigate his malpractice cause of action in the plaintiff physician's suit for fees, or vice versa, in spite of the majority position that a physician's action for fees and a patient's medical malpractice action are distinct and independent, and collateral estoppel should not be applicable.[428]

9.3 MASS ACCIDENTS AND CLASS ACTIONS

Mass accidents bring forth multiple plaintiffs, and the rush to judgment frequently works an injustice, as where the first plaintiff loses and the winning defendant seeks to preclude relitigation of the liability issue in subsequent suits brought by other plaintiffs. This defensive collateral estoppel[429] is said to decrease litigation, but it obviously deprives other plaintiffs of their day in court. On the other hand, offensive collateral estoppel,[430] should the defendant win in the first suit, may tend to increase litigation, for the mass tort plaintiff has a strong incentive to avoid joinder and await the successful outcome of litigation commenced by other multiple plaintiffs; the defendant may be sued repeatedly by multiple plaintiffs. Another objection to offensive collateral estoppel is that a plaintiff can unfairly bind a defendant whose loss in the first suit may have been caused by tactical disadvantages[431] rather than by weakness in defendant's case. Offensive collateral estoppel may be unfair to a defendant who refrained from offering a vigorous defense in the prior trial because the damages sought were minimal, as shown in Berner v. British Commonwealth Pacific Airlines, Ltd.,[432] where the prior action terminated in a judgment adverse to the airline in the amount of $35,000 when the potential liability ran into the millions of dollars. Offensive collateral estoppel might be unfair or even unjust where the defendant in the second suit desires to avail himself of procedural opportunities not afforded in the first suit, as illustrated in Parklane Hosiery Co. v. Shore.[433] Also, offensive collateral estoppel could allow a plaintiff to rely upon a judgment against a defendant even if inconsistent with judgments previously rendered for the defendant. The thrust of these objections to offensive collateral estoppel is especially acute in mass tort situations where the multiple plaintiffs reside in different jurisdictions and their injuries involved different circumstances, and the common defendant or defendants are deprived of a full and fair opportunity to litigate. Indeed, the great weight of judicial authority stands for the proposition that collateral estoppel should not be applied in mass accident litigation.[434]

Mass accidents give rise to class actions, although in 1966 one authority exclaimed that

> a mass accident resulting in injuries to numerous persons is ordinarily not appropriate for a class action because of the likelihood that significant questions, not only of damages, but of liability and defenses to liability, would be present, affecting the individuals in different ways. In these circumstances an action conducted nominally as a class action would degenerate in practice into multiple lawsuits separately tried.[435]

Fortunately, this dire prediction does not ring true, for class actions have been certified readily and have resulted in judicial economy and even plaintiff satisfaction. Rule 23 (c) (4) (A) of the Federal Rules of Civil Procedure (FRCP), for example, "allows an action to be maintained as a class action with respect to particular issues where appropriate and does not require that all liability issues in an action be determinable on a class-wide basis before the action may be certified as a class action."[436] The same federal district court in Pennsylvania concluded that "class certification may not be denied simply because an action may be called a 'mass tort'. The factual and legal issues specific to the particular litigation must be analyzed to determine whether class certification is proper under Rule 23 and offers a superior method for the fair and efficient adjudication of the controversy."[437]

Some courts have ruled that res judicata or collateral estoppel does not bar individualized claims which were expressly not litigated in the prior class action litigation, even if the claims arose out of the same basic allegations of wrongful activity or violation of law. These courts rely on the traditional argument that only claims actually litigated or only claims that might have been litigated are precluded by an earlier adjudication between the parties.[438] In Edwards v. Boeing Vertol Co.[439] the Third U.S. Court of Appeals found res judicata to be inapplicable:

> The judgment in the class action determined no more than that the class representatives had failed to prove a company-wide pattern or practice of discrimination. Edwards is not, however, attempting to relitigate what was finally determined in the class action. The trial court explicitly held that its decision in favor of the employer was not a determination that individual employees had not been victims of discrimination. . . . The class action judgment is not a former adjudication.

Indeed,

> clients who have claims not raised in this class action because claims are unsuitable for class treatment, can bring those claims on an individual basis, and Res Judicata will not bar those claims because absent class members had no opportunity to litigate those issues in this lawsuit.[440]

Indeed, courts can separate counts of a complaint; "some counts may proceed for the class while others go forward only for named plaintiffs."[441] The U.S. Supreme Court in Cooper v. Federal Reserve Bank of Richmond[442] emphasized in 1984 that res judicata would not apply to any claim unless the lower court had specifically adjudicated that claim in the context of the class action. The thrust of the law is that a party in a class action context must have a full and fair opportunity to litigate a particular issue if he is to be precluded from subsequently asserting that particular issue.

The U.S. Supreme Court in the Parklane Hosiery case[443] indicated in 1979 a trend toward requiring intervention, joinder, or some other consolidation of all parties into one case. Twelve years earlier the highest court in Provident

Tradesmen's Bank & Trust Co. v. Patterson[444] recognized that intervention was an important tool to help courts save time and prevent multiple litigation; consolidation of multiple cases would assure consistent judgments and minimize relitigation.[445]

9.4 ADMINISTRATIVE AGENCIES

Administrative law must grapple not only with the special problems growing out of differences between the judicial process and the administrative process, but also with the problem of res judicata or collateral estoppel, both of which preclusive devices were designed for adjudication typified by a court proceeding. Courts normally apply the law to facts that are past and static, whereas administrative agencies often work with fluid facts and shifting political and economic policies; permitting a "second chance" in an administrative agency proceeding may be justifiable, but in a court of law the termination of the controversy mandates just "one bite out of the apple." The finality of unappealed judgments of courts is ordinarily well understood, but finality of administrative hearings and rulings is seldom clear and frequently invites re-argument and rehearings.

The U.S. Supreme Court in United States v. Utah Construction & Mining Co.[446] had occasion to remark in 1966 that

> occasionally courts have used language to the effect that res judicata principles do not apply to administrative proceedings, but such language is certainly too broad. When an administrative agency is acting in a judicial capacity and resolves disputed issues of fact properly before it which the parties have had an adequate opportunity to litigate, the courts have not hesitated to apply res judicata to enforce repose. . . .

In Continental Can Co. v. Marshall[447] the Seventh U.S. Court of Appeals in 1979 analyzed three issues regarding the application of collateral estoppel to the administrative proceedings which resulted in the manufacturer facing numerous citations regarding noise levels at its eighty plants: (1) whether the preclusive device elements of identity of parties and identity of issues were met; (2) whether the plaintiff had to exhaust all administrative remedies before obtaining judicial relief; and (3) whether denial of the preclusive device would place undue hardship upon plaintiff so as to justify injunctive relief by the court. The court, in granting relief, found that full and fair opportunity to litigate had been timely, and the manufacturer was able to avoid untold litigation expenses. On the other hand, in Western Oil & Gas Association v. Environmental Protection Agency (EPA)[448] the Ninth U.S. Court of Appeals ruled that the EPA was not barred from relitigating the issue of air quality control standards since California's air quality control standards were unique and independent of findings of other states. But federal administrative agencies have been barred from relitigating issues previously litigated in state agency proceedings, as illustrated by United States v. ITT Rayonier, Inc.,[449] where the EPA sought an enforcement of water pollution discharge permits, but was frustrated by the prior determination of the issue by the Washington Department of Ecology, a state agency that was ''sufficiently close'' to the federal EPA.

Administrative agencies may even get second cracks at offenders engaged in wrongful practices, as illustrated by the 1942 U.S. Supreme Court determination in Federal Trade Commission (FTC) v. Raladam Co.[450] In 1929 the FTC had found that the defendant had used unfair methods of competition in selling its fat-reducing product, but the highest court then affirmed a judgment setting aside the FTC cease and desist order on the ground of lack of evidence of injury to competitors. In 1935 the FTC instituted new proceedings against the defendant after making the required finding of injury to competitors, and the defendant contended that res judicata should be applied to bar the proceedings. But the highest court ruled that the FTC was not barred:

> The reasons for refusing to enforce the Commission's order are grounded upon inadequacy of the findings and proof as revealed in the particular record then before this Court. Hence, these reasons are not controlling in this case, arising, as it does, out of different proceedings and presenting different facts and a different record for our consideration.

However, where it is important to give preclusive effect to an administrative decision to preserve its finality, the court will do so, as shown in the 1940 case of Sunshine Anthracite Coal Co. v. Adkins:[451] here a decision of one agency was held binding on the government for the purposes of a later case before another agency. And in United States v. Jan Hardware Manufacturing Co.[452] the defendant was assessed a monetary penalty by one agency and when defendant failed to pay, the government sued in the federal district court to collect the penalty. The court held that defendant was collaterally estopped from arguing that the government had failed to prove the violations and that the particular statute was constitutional, all in the interest of protecting the finality of the administrative determination.

The doctrine of collateral estoppel was held to be inapplicable in Young & Company v. Shea,[453] where Tugwell sued a shipowner for injuries received aboard defendant's ship and the shipowner impleaded Young, the employer of Tugwell; the jury found no injury, and then Tugwell sought compensation under the Longshoremen's and Harbor Workers' Act, and his employer moved to dismiss on the basis of the jury verdict that Tugwell sustained no injury. Nevertheless, the commissioner made an award: ''The fact that a worker could not convince a jury that he had suffered an injury should not estop him from attempting to convince a Commissioner that he was injured inasmuch as the standard of persuasion is less before the Commissioner than before the court.''[454] Indeed, there must be flexibility in applying the preclusive devices to administrative agencies; as stated by Professor Kenneth Davis in his Administrative Law text; competing interests should be weighed by courts such as the statute which created the agency.[455] Some administrative determinations are without preclusive devices because of the high degree of fluidity required for a particular function of the agency; other administrative action requires modification or relaxation of preclusion so that an earlier decision will not be binding. A fitting example is found in New York State Labor Relations Board v. Holland Laundry, Inc.,[456] where no preclusive effect was given to a judgment of the New York court adjudging the employer not guilty of unfair labor practices in a subsequent proceeding brought before the board by the union on other charges of unfair labor practices. As indicated in Miller v. Poretsky,[457] federal courts are reluctant to apply res judicata or collateral estoppel to prior state determination in civil rights litigation, although congressional policy is to achieve a national uniform result in civil rights enforcement, but not at the expense of individual rights. On the other hand, in Bowen v. United States,[458] the Seventh U.S. Court of Appeals said that enough was enough and precluded the plaintiff from further litigation; here plaintiff crashed his plane, and the agency suspended his license for thirty days; he appealed to another agency, which found that he had violated regulations of the first agency, although the suspension order was reduced to fifteen days; then plaintiff sued the United States, alleging failure of another agency to warn him about a danger that allegedly caused his plane to crash. But the court ruled that the prior determination precluded his suit, and the appellate court affirmed: ''Issue preclusion applies to a final administrative determination of an issue properly before an agency acting in a judicial capacity when both parties were aware of the possible significance of that issue in later proceedings and were afforded a full opportunity to litigate that issue and obtain judicial review.''[459]

The decision in Matter of Waterside Associates (New York State Department of Environmental Conservation)[460] presented an estoppel issue that was ''novel and one of apparent first impression.'' Three years after initially designating portions of thirty-seven acres in Staten Island as having ''wetland status,'' the New York State Department of Environmental Conservation (DEC) was estopped to cite the possible extension of that status to other parts of the tract as a basis for blocking a planned housing development in the area. The New York Supreme Court, Richmond County, was aware that the doctrine of collateral estoppel does not apply to actions taken by the government in the exercise of its police powers;[461] but the court found that Section 24-0703 (5) of the New York Environmental Conservation Law waived the state's claim to protection by setting time frames within which the state must respond to requests whether an area will be designated as a ''wetland'': ''[The statutory provision] is a clear and unmistakeable expression that the state has waived its immunity from equitable principles of estoppel against the exercise of its sovereign powers.'' The New York court further opined that the doctrine of estoppel may also be invoked against the government in the exercise of its sovereign or governmental powers where there has been justifiable reliance on the part of the party who seeks to invoke it. . . . The petitioners were unquestionably justified in relying on the contents of the Colvin letter. . . . Nothing in the letter reserved any rights to redesignate the property as a freshwater wetland. . . . Petitioners relied on the letter to their financial detriment in that they purchased the subject parcels for over three million dollars. . . . Substantial expenditures made in reliance upon an act of municipality may be the basis for an estoppel if the act is not clearly beyond the scope of the municipality's authority. . . . If the DEC were permitted to ignore the effect of the Colvin letter, . . . a manifest injustice would result. . . .

9.5 GOVERNMENTS

It has been said that governments may not be estopped nor precluded by the acts or omissions of their officials or agents, but that reference is subsumed under the general doctrine of sovereign immunity, which has generally been relaxed in recent years. Yet in 1947 in Federal Crop Insurance Corp. v. Merrill[462] the U.S. Supreme Court refused to preclude the federal government, despite the fact that its agent had insured defendant's reseeded spring wheat, perhaps not realizing that the federal regulations precluded insurance for reseeded spring wheat: "Anyone entering into an arrangement with the Government takes the risk of having accurately ascertained that he who purports to act for the Government stays within the bounds of his authority."[463] In 1984 in Heckler v. Community Health Services[464] a government agent incorrectly advised the defendant about Medicare reimbursements, and when the government sought to recoup overpayments of more than $63,000, the defendant argued that the government was estopped from recovering the overpayments because of the affirmative misconduct of the government agent. Although the Third U.S. Court of Appeals was willing to estop the government,[465] the U.S. Supreme Court reversed, finding that defendant had failed to demonstrate that the traditional elements of estoppel were present. Also, "when the government is unable to enforce the law because the conduct of its agents has given rise to an estoppel, the interest of the citizenry as a whole in obedience to the rule of law is undermined. It is for this reason that it is well-settled that the Government may not be estopped on the same terms as any other litigant."[466] Earlier in 1981 in Schweiker v. Hansen[467] the highest court observed that the government field representative for Social Security had erred in believing that plaintiff was not eligible for benefits; plaintiff, now eligible, sought retroactive benefits, but the court ruled that the government agent's error fell far short of the kind of misconduct required to estop the government. Affirmative misconduct on the part of a government official or agent must be more than a mere oversight,[468] as illustrated in Lurch v. United States,[469] where the plaintiff sued for medical malpractice at a Veterans Administration (VA) hospital; in a separate Freedom of Information Act suit the government contended that the surgery was performed by staff surgeons at the VA hospital. Later plaintiff learned that the surgery was actually performed by an independent contracting surgeon, but plaintiff had no knowledge of this fact until after the statute of limitations had expired. The court ruled that the government was not estopped from asserting the physician's independent-contractor status; there was no showing that the government had acted in such a way that plaintiff had the right to believe the physician was a governmental employee, and there was no proof of affirmative misconduct on the part of the government.

In Young v. United States[470] offensive collateral estoppel was refused in an action brought against the federal government under its swine flu vaccination program. Evidently an earlier proceeding under Ohio law resulted in a finding that the warnings on the serum and the consent form were inadequate; but the government was not estopped to relitigate the adequacy of the warnings and the consent form in New York. Similarly, an acquittal in a criminal action, although a valid and final judgment, will not collaterally estop the government from relitigating an issue in a subsequent civil suit where the burden of proof required is less, as shown in One Lot Emerald Cut Stone and One Ring v. United States[471].

Plaintiffs brought survival and wrongful death actions against the United States in a federal district court in Maryland in Gliedman v. Capital Airlines, Inc.[472] A collision occurred in the air space over Maryland between a jet trainer consigned to the Maryland National Guard and the defendant airline jet. An earlier proceeding in the District of Columbia had found the United States negligent, and the court here ruled that the earlier judgment in favor of the plaintiffs collaterally estopped the United States from relitigating the issue of negligence.[473] The contrary view is seen in Bruszewski v. United States,[474] which involved an action by a longshoreman against the federal government for injury suffered while he was working on a docked ship owned by the federal government and serviced by a private corporation. The government pleaded res judicata on the strength of a judgment against the plaintiff and in favor of the private corporation. The Third U.S. Court of Appeals pointed out that a finding of negligence in the earlier case would not have a binding effect on the United States since the government had no opportunity to contest the issues in the first suit; and therefore no unfairness would result from the lack of preclusion.

Estoppel was denied against "a subsidiary corporation of a public authority" in Albano v. The Long Island Railroad Co.[475] The plaintiff had apparently not complied with Section 1276 (1) of the New York Public Authorities Law with respect to giving thirty days' notice of suit. But plaintiff amended the complaint to comply with the statute; and defendant did nothing for over two years, so that the trial court found that "defendant was equitably estopped by its silence for over two years following joinder of issue from asserting plaintiff's failure to comply with the demand requirements of Public Authorities Law Section 1276 (1)." The New York Appellate Division, Second Dept., disagreed, and found no estoppel because of the general rule that collateral estoppel is inapplicable to government subdivisions acting in their governmental capacity.

9.6 ARBITRATION

Arbitration, the nonjudicial, contractual method of resolving disputes, is also a vehicle for the preclusion devices of res judicata and collateral estoppel.[476] In Ritchie v. Landau[477] a lawyer employed by a corporation claimed entitlement to a substantial bonus for certain recoveries he had obtained for his employer. In accord with his contract of employment he first sought the monies in an arbitration proceeding, and he was successful in recovering only 10 percent of the monies allegedly due him. He then sued the corporation's principal stockholder, but the federal district court dismissed his suit on grounds of collateral estoppel, and the Second U.S. Court of Appeals affirmed, pointing out that the principal stockholder was not a party to the initial arbitration proceedings! A federal district court in New York in Ufheil Construction Co. v. Town of New Windsor,[478] four years later, was unwilling to accept another plaintiff's argument that an earlier arbitration award collaterally estopped the defendant from relitigating issues that were addressed in the award; the court ruled that the arbitrator's award was too ambiguous and the issues addressed in the arbitration were unclear, and therefore collateral estoppel would be inapplicable.[479]

It should be observed that for the preclusive device to be applicable to the arbitration proceeding, the determination in arbitration must have been essential to the award.[480] In Matter of Guarantee Insurance Company (D'Alleva)[481] the operator of a motor vehicle in New York had been denied no-fault benefits under New York law on the ground that he had been intoxicated at the time of the accident, but the no-fault arbitrator found that the operator had not been intoxicated at the time of the accident, and that the other vehicle was at fault. The operator then sought arbitration of an uninsured motorist's claim, and the same insurer moved to stay the arbitration proceeding pending judicial determination as to whether there had been contact with the other vehicle. The claimant contended that the arbitrator's finding concerning the other vehicle collaterally estopped the insurer from endeavoring to relitigate that issue. The New York Appellate Division, First Dept., rejected the preclusive device, pointing out that in the first arbitration proceeding the only issue was whether the operator was intoxicated at the time of the accident, and that the abitrator's gratuitous finding that the other vehicle was at fault was not essential to that determination and therefore could not serve as the basis for collateral estoppel.

On the other hand, in Brown v. Moore[482] the New York Appellate Division, Second Dept., in 1986 ruled that plaintiff was collaterally estopped from relitigating defendant's involvement in the automobile accident, for the record indicated that that issue had been resolved in the defendant's favor in an arbitration proceeding: "The mere fact that the Motor Vehicle Accident Information Corporation is also a defendant here, having intervened in this action, does not affect defendant Moore's right to have plaintiff's action against her dismissed on the ground of collateral estoppel.'' Plaintiff sued the owner of a vehicle who claimed that her vehicle had been stolen prior to the accident and that she was therefore not responsible for the personal injuries arising from the collision. While this personal injury action was pending plaintiff filed an uninsured motorist's claim based upon defendant's allegation that her vehicle had been stolen prior to the accident or collision. The arbitration proceeding resulted in an award of $10,000 in favor of the plaintiff. The defendant then moved in court to dismiss the personal injuries action on the ground that plaintiff was collaterally estopped from contending that her vehicle was operated with her permission when the arbitration proceeding confirmed the fact that her vehicle was operated without her permission. The court dismissed the complaint, even though the court remarked that ''defendant's reliance upon the doctrine of collateral estoppel or issue preclusion is misplaced'' because there was no full and fair opportunity for both parties to litigate the salient issue; however, plaintiff's action was barred here under the guise of ''collateral estoppel against inconsistent positions.''

9.7 TAX FRAUDS

The tremendous volume of cases concerned with tax frauds has resulted in greater judicial use of preclusive devices to achieve finality.[483] Typically in statutory actions courts have applied collateral estoppel automatically after a conviction under a related statute, as illustrated by Gray v. Commissioner of Internal Revenue,[484] where conviction for criminal tax evasion was determinative of the fraud element of a civil tax fraud. The inquiry is whether a given fact or given issue has been judicially determined in the prior proceeding, although many tax statutes provide for both criminal and civil liability, as shown in Section 7201 of the Internal Revenue Code (IRC), which states that ''any person who willfully attempts in any manner to evade or defeat any tax imposed by this title or the payment thereof shall, in addition to other penalties provided by law, be guilty of a felony and, upon conviction thereof, shall be fined . . . or imprisoned. . . . ''[485] On the other hand, an acquittal in a criminal action, although a valid and final judgment, will not collaterally estop the government from relitigating an issue in a subsequent civil suit; in Neaderland v. Commission[486] the Second U.S. Court of Appeals refused to apply collateral estoppel because the criminal and civil fraud actions required different burdens of proof.

In general, it can be stated that in tax fraud decisions courts have applied the preclusive devices mechanically and not consistently with equitable considerations.[487] For example, a finding of essential identity of issues is based on a comparison of the willfulness requirement of the criminal tax fraud statute (Section 7201 of IRC) and the fraud requirement of the civil penalty provision (Section 6653(b) of IRC). Yet there can be little doubt that between the two statutes there are solid differences in sanctions, character, and language as well as the constantly changing nature of the subject matter, the use of a different accounting period, and the undesirable result of a perpetuation of an erroneous tax court decision over a number of years.[488] In Amos v. Commissioner of Internal Revenue[489] the Tax Court ruled that a finding of willfulness was equivalent to a finding of fraud, thus satisfying the collateral estoppel requisite of identity of issues. But where there is a negotiated guilty plea in the criminal action for tax fraud the identity of issues may be obfuscated, and furthermore there may have been no actual adjudication of the issue; indeed, the issue to be collaterally estopped must at least have been raised in pleadings and other evidence.[490] Yet in Arctic Ice Cream Co. v. Commissioner of Internal Revenue[491] the Tax Court's analysis suggests that because a guilty plea reflects guilt, i.e., the defendant presumably admits that the charge of tax fraud is true, it is unnecessary to look at the pleadings or other evidence to predicate actual adjudication. A criminal conviction for tax fraud is a valid and final judgment regardless of whether it is based on a judgment after trial or on a negotiated guilty plea.[492]

9.8 CRIMINAL CONDUCT AND CRIMINAL PROCEEDINGS

It is well established that resolution of issues of criminal conduct in criminal proceedings may be a basis of res judicata or collateral estoppel in subsequent civil proceedings.[493] But the acceptance of this principle depends on the verdict reached in the criminal proceeding, the type of court which heard the subsequent civil action, the protections afforded the criminal defendant, including Fifth Amendment rights,[494] and generally whether full and fair opportunity to be heard was accorded the defendant. In Mueller v. J. C. Penney Co.[495] the plaintiff left defendant's store with unpaid cosmetics in her handbag and was apprehended by defendant's security guard; a fight broke out and plaintiff was arrested by the police. Plaintiff thereupon sued the defendant for assault and battery (her husband joined for loss of consortium); but in the interim plaintiff was convicted of misdemeanor charges arising out of the shoplifting incident. The California trial court gave collateral estoppel effect to plaintiff's criminal conviction, and the jury found for the defendant. The California appellate court affirmed, finding that the issue decided in the misdemeanor criminal case was identical to the issue to be relitigated in the civil suit: the misdemeanor finding was a final judgment, free from direct attack and immune from reversal or amendment, because the plaintiff had the incentive to litigate fully the misdemeanor charge and had a full and fair opportunity to pursue her defense at trial.

In Re Raiford[496] the Eleventh U.S. Court of Appeals ruled that a debtor's guilty plea and conviction to a bankruptcy crime estopped him from relitigating factual issues in common between the criminal statute and the bankruptcy statute, and he was therefore denied a discharge of indebtedness under Chapter 11 of the Bankruptcy Code.[497] The court must scrutinize the record of the criminal proceeding in order to determine specifically what issues were decided.[498] The

New York Court of Appeals in its 1980 decision in People v. Berkowitz[499] rejected defendant's argument that the prior acquittal of his alleged co-conspirator in a criminal trial collaterally estopped the government from trying him on the same charge of conspiracy; the court distinguished between the degree of accuracy necessary in criminal as opposed to civil litigation, and perhaps cynically portrayed the obfuscation of issues in the subsequent civil action.[500] In Travelers Insurance Co. v. Thompson[501] the Minnesota court held that the prior criminal conviction was inadmissible hearsay evidence in the later civil suit because the jurors in the criminal case lacked personal knowledge required of witnesses permitted to testify! The acquittal of an IRS agent charged with receiving unlawful gratuities did not preclude the government from prosecuting the person who was charged with aiding and abetting the IRS agent in Standefer v. United States:[502] here the highest court reasoned that the government was without a full and fair opportunity to litigate the criminal case since it had limited discovery rights, and summary procedures like directed verdicts are seldom available to the government; and furthermore, policy interests in the enforcement of criminal law outweigh the economic considerations underlying the use of collateral estoppel in subsequent actions.[503] But the government was estopped in United States v. Abatti,[504] where the federal district court in California ruled that a favorable civil judgment on a taxpayer's petition for redetermination of his tax liability precluded the government's criminal prosecution of the taxpayer for tax evasion and submission of false tax return.

The fact that the finality of an issue in a prior criminal action may bind the party or parties in a subsequent civil suit has had an interesting result, to wit: non-parties are encouraged to participate in the criminal proceeding. A potential defendant in the subsequent civil suit may be encouraged to underwrite the expense of a criminal defendant's trial, as where the corporation may be precluded due to the criminal conviction of its employee, as in In Re Teltronics, Inc.,[505] where the Seventh U.S. Court of Appeals ruled that the mail fraud conviction of a principal officer collaterally estopped the corporation from contesting the existence of fraud in the subsequent civil aciton. Even an insurance company may prefer to enter the fray early and provide the criminal defendant with an attorney because of the likely civil suit that follows.[506] In Hurtt v. Stirone[507] the Pennsylvania Supreme Court held that a person convicted of extortion could not relitigate questions concerning his conduct in a subsequent civil action in a state court to recover the monies extorted; to ignore the effect of the prior jury determination of his guilt for the crime of extortion would "fly in the face of reason and be a general indictment of the whole American jury system."[508] Courts do not restrict the government's use of offensive collateral estoppel to suits for recovery of the fruits of a crime, as illustrated by Securities and Exchange Commission v. Everest Management Corp.,[509] where the court enjoined the defendant from filing false securities statements and from executing a fraudulent bank transaction after the principal defendant had been criminally convicted of securities violations stemming from the same transaction that precipitated the civil suit. Courts have granted private plaintiffs summary judgment against defendants convicted of filing false financial reports in violation of securities laws.[510] In Travelers Indemnity Co. v. Walburn[511] the court granted the insurance company's motion for summary judgment against the insured, who was convicted of murder, so that the insurer was relieved of its obligation to defend a wrongful death suit brought against the murderer!

The potential application of the preclusive devices in the subsequent civil suit may invite the crime of perjury, as demonstrated in United States v. Frank,[512] where the Second U.S. Court of Appeals acknowledged that the trend toward wider application of res judicata and collateral estoppel "may subject complaining witnesses in federal criminal trials to more severe attacks on credibility than would otherwise be the case. Arguably, and perhaps more seriously, it provides too tempting a reward for overstatement or even perjury." The possibility that someone stands to benefit from the criminal conviction and will commit perjury strikes at the very heart and integrity of criminal proceedings. Interestingly, courts have refused to grant relief in civil suits for perjury upon grounds of res judicata and collateral estoppel; as stated in Smith v. Sinclair,[513] "It is fundamental that in the absence of statute an unsuccessful litigant may not maintain a civil suit for damages against a person for alleged perjury committed by him in a civil action, a criminal prosecution, or other proceeding, either as a party or as a witness."[514] The reasons for the rule against civil actions for perjury are many, to wit: witnesses are encouraged to speak freely in court since they are protected from subsequently being sued for perjury;[515] criminal sanctions provide a sufficient deterrent to false testimony;[516] and the necessity for finality of verdicts and judgments.[517] The preclusive effects are vividly shown in an 1808 New York decision of Smith v. Lewis,[518] where plaintiff sued defendant, contending that as a result of defendant's perjured testimony in a Connecticut court, plaintiff was found guilty of land fraud in the prior suit in Connecticut. The New York court applied the preclusion of res judicata: "If maintainable, there will be no end to litigation. It will again be trying the same cause. . . . The verdict can never be inquired into, in this way, by a collateral suit. The judgment of the court must be considered final and conclusive. Res Judicata pro veritate accipitur." (A thing adjudged is taken as true.)[519]

10

Preclusions of All Sorts and Sizes and Shapes

The preclusive doctrines of res judicata and collateral estoppel represent the totality of preclusions, but there are innumerable instances beyond those delineated in Chapter 9 herein which have important roles to play in the scheme of adjudication. Res judicata, for example, can be subdivided into the two closely related doctrines of merger and bar, the former applying when a claimant has prevailed in the earlier action and the latter applying when a claimant has lost in the earlier action. When a claimant wins a judgment in the first suit, all possible grounds for the winning cause of action are said to be ''merged'' into that judgment and are not available for further litigation. If the claimant loses the first suit, he is said to be ''barred'' by the adverse judgment from ever raising the same cause of action again, even if he can present new grounds for recovery. For example, a plaintiff who was injured in an automobile accident sues the defendant, alleging injury to his right arm, and he loses the case when the jury finds that he was contributorily negligent. Should the same plaintiff subsequently file a second suit claiming injury to his left arm from the same accident, the earlier adverse decision will serve to ''bar'' his subsequent suit since it is based on the same cause of action. On the other hand, if the plaintiff prevailed in the first suit and recovered damages for injury to his right arm and now files a subsequent suit for damages for injury to his left arm, the original judgment will preclude the subsequent suit because the second claim had ''merged'' into the first suit, and plaintiff cannot ''split his cause of action.''

There is a close relationship between double jeopardy in the criminal suit and res judicata in the civil suit, the former prohibiting repeated prosecution of criminal charges, and the latter prohibiting repeated civil claims.[520] But double jeopardy does not wait for finality such as a valid judgment on the merits, for double jeopardy attaches to a criminal proceeding when the accused is in imminent danger of conviction, at which point the prosecution cannot renew the same charges in a second proceeding no matter how the case develops in the first court. Indeed, double jeopardy is deemed to have attached when the jury is sworn or when a witness is examined; should the prosecution be dismissed before the jury is impanelled, the accused has not been placed in double jeopardy and the criminal charges can be refiled.

Still another preclusive doctrine is the Law of the Case, which delineates the principle that issues once decided in a case cannot be redetermined, should the same issues recur later in the proceedings. The U.S. Supreme Court in Messinger v. Anderson[521] tersely described the Law of the Case as "merely expressing the practice of courts generally to refuse to reopen what has been decided, not a limit on their power."

Hereinanfter set forth is a motley collection of preclusions necessary to complete the picture of res judicata and collateral estoppel "in action," to wit: estoppel by deed (Section 10.1); corporation and/or partnership by estoppel (Section 10.2); estoppel by record (Section 10.3); estoppel against estoppel (Section 10.4); election of remedies (Section 10.5); compulsory counterclaim (Section 10.6); stay of proceedings (Section 10.7); judgment on the merits (Section 10.8); substantive relationship (Section 10.9); and total res judicata (Section 10.10).

10.1 ESTOPPEL BY DEED

Estoppel by deed is a bar which precludes a party from denying the truth of his deed in a suit on the deed or in a suit concerning a right arising out of the deed. One aim of estoppel by deed is to avoid circuity of action and at the same time compel the parties to fulfill their contracts.[522] But estoppel by deed is not created or enforceable unless there has been a change in the situation of one of the parties in reliance on the deed,[523] as illustrated by John & Sal's Automotive Service, Inc. v. Montesano,[524] where the grantee was estopped to contend that the covenants in the deed were not covenants running with the land and were not binding on his grantees; here the grantee had originally agreed that covenants in the deed that gasoline, oil, and petroleum products of the grantor would be used on the demised premises for a fifteen-year term, would run with the land and be binding on any grantee of the grantee; obviously, the parties had changed positions in reliance on the deed.

Estoppel has been frequently raised against a grantor who asserts anything in derogation of his deed. The grantor will not be heard to say, for the purpose of defeating the title of the grantee, that at the time of the conveyance he had no title or that none passed by the deed, nor can the grantor deny to the deed its full operation and effect as a conveyance.[525] In Harrell v. Powell[526] the North Carolina court ruled that where property held by husband and wife was conveyed to a third person by a deed executed by only one spouse, the surviving spouse, on the death of the other spouse, was estopped to dispute the validity of the deed on the ground that the other spouse did not join in the conveyance. A grantee by accepting a deed, however, is not estopped to deny his grantor's title, except where he relies on such grantor's conveyance to establish his own claim. It is common sense that one asserting title under a deed is estopped to deny the validity of the deed at the same time he is asserting ownership by virtue of the deed.[527] Similar rules apply to the mortgagor and the mortgagee with respect to estoppel by deed. On the other hand, it was part of the doctrine of estoppel by deed that, although the facts recited in the deed could not be contradicted by the parties, the acts could be contradicted by third persons "who, if it were otherwise, might be prejudiced by things recited in the writings, contrary to the truth, through the ignorance, carelessness, or fraud of the parties; and who, therefore, ought not to be precluded from proving the truth, however contradictory to the written statements of others."[528] Indeed, the parole evidence rule is applicable only to the parties to the deed and their privies, but does not apply to third persons unless the third persons are endeavoring to enforce rights under the deed.[529]

Contracts which purport to convey interests in real property not then owned by the seller are often dealt with under the concept of estoppel by deed. According to one legal scholar, "[T]here are decisions and numerous dicta to the effect, not only that the grantor in a conveyance is estopped to deny that it passed the estate which it purported to pass, but also that the conveyance actually passes, by way of estoppel, any estate or title which the grantor may thereafter acquire in land, if this is within its apparent scope."[530] Where facts relating to title are peculiarly within the knowledge of one against whom an estoppel is claimed, mere silence is enough to work an estoppel by deed.[531] Where reasonable diligence by the purchaser might have guarded against loss, as where the title is fully recorded, something in the way of fraud or encouragement beyond mere silence is requisite to work an estoppel.[532] In both instances, the estoppel rests on the owner's conduct, which amounts to a misrepresentation of an existing fact.

Another interesting aspect of the estoppel by deed arises in connection with an action to recover rentals from the defendant, as shown in Title Guarantee & Trust Co. v. Monson,[533] where a judgment in a prior action for specific performance awarded possession of the land to the plaintiff. The defendant urged that the prior action was a bar to further proceedings as the claim for rent collected by defendant could have been litigated in the prior action. The California court held that the action for rents collected was not a necessary or indispensable issue in the prior action, and refused estoppel by deed because the two suits arose from different rights: the action for specific performance was based upon contract provisions in a deed of trust, while the action to recover rents collected by defendant was based on his wrongful act in collecting rents which belonged to plaintiff. An earlier California case, Denning v. Green,[534] prompted the court to declare that in the first suit to quiet title "there is no mention of rental in the conclusions of law or in the judgment. The evidence in the former case is not before us. It thus appears, and we must conclude that the matter of rental was not an issue in the case. Matters not in issue in the previous action are not Res Judicata (or Estoppel by Deed).''

10.2 CORPORATION AND/OR PARTNERSHIP BY ESTOPPEL

Collateral attack on corporations or partnerships is frequent and is the cause of much enmity between attorneys representing stockholders especially and attorneys defending corporations or partnerships. ''Corporation by estoppel'' serves to protect the interests of the corporation (or partnership) where the necessary elements of ''holding out'' as a corporation (or partnership) and of ''reliance'' upon the fact of corporation (or partnership) are present. Of course, where there is no de jure corporation (or partnership) and the defects are so serious as to preclude application of the de facto doctrine,[535] the preclusion devices of res judicata or collateral estoppel may not be invoked.[536] Third parties, associates, and the purported corporation or partnership itself may each be subject to preclusion. One who has dealt with a purported corporation or purported partnership may be estopped from denying the existence of the corporation or partnership; persons who held themselves out as a corporation or partnership may be estopped from claiming otherwise.[537]

An ostensible partner in a partnership who represents himself or consents to be represented as a partner may be liable as a partner to any person who, on the strength of such representation, has given credit to the partnership, for example. The true partner or partners, if they consented to the representations, may be liable also to third parties for the acts of the ostensible partner to the same extent as if the ostensible partner were a true partner.[538] A corporation, using a company name not including corporateness but perhaps a partnership, may be treated as a ''partnership by estoppel'' where a third party with which the company deals has neither the knowledge nor notice of such incorporation.[539]

When a corporation incorporated in one jurisdiction does business in another jurisdiction but fails to be admitted or to qualify to do business in that other jurisdiction, that other jurisdiction may impose personal liability on officers, directors, and agents of the corporation.[540]

10.3 ESTOPPEL BY RECORD

Generally estoppel by record exists only between the same parties or those in legal privity with them, and cannot be invoked by one who is himself not bound thereby.[541] Estoppel by record bars a second action on an issue necessarily raised and decided in the first suit. But there can be no estoppel by record where the allegations were immaterial[542] or where they were made through inadvertence or by mistake.[543] Where the files of the prior suit were missing and it was impossible to determine with any degree of certainty what the issues in the first suit were, that first suit cannot serve as the basis for estoppel by record in the subsequent suit.[544]

A judgment is a record that can give rise to an estoppel, especially the default judgment which is generally entered without a contest on the merits and which can be binding in subsequent suits on the same cause of action. A default judgment against the superintendent of a club was deemed conclusive in a subsequent suit for an accounting brought against the superintendent by the club members.[545] A default judgment in favor of the plaintiff in a suit to recover payment on certain notes was conclusive on the question of the validity of the debt in a subsequent suit involving the same parties.[546] In essence, a default judgment determines issues pleaded and necessary to the judgment, and thus gives rise to estoppel by record. In Wolcott v. Hutchins[547] the Second U.S. Court of Appeals intimated that "the present proceeding appears to be one more step in an apparently endless saga generated by David's determination to prosecute a thoroughly, and repeatedly, discredited claim," and the court concluded:

> We are dealing with Estoppel by Judgment that concludes the parties, both as to those matters actually litigated and those which might have been raised with respect to the same cause of action. . . . In the present case, plaintiff alleges that he has suffered the identical injury which he charged in the prior action. However, he is seeking to avoid the bar by pointing out that the means by which defendant inflicted the injury are different. Stripped of verbiage the substance of David's prior and present causes of action, however, is one and the same.

The judgment, whether default or not, estops by virtue of the record any relitigation of the same cause of action. An unappealed declaratory judgment declaring the rights and legal relations of the parties to a pension agreement was effective and binding on the parties, when subsequently an appellate court decision involving other parties decided that the prior declaratory judgment was an error of law. The Rhode Island Supreme Court in Lopes v. Mallory[548] held that the unappealed declaratory judgment in the earlier suit "stands as a final judgment, rendered on the merits, without fraud or collusion, by a court of competent jurisdiction. This judgment is conclusive of rights, questions, and facts in issue, as to the parties and their privies in all other judicial tribunals of concurrent jurisdiction."[549]

10.4 ESTOPPEL AGAINST ESTOPPEL

An estoppel against estoppel is perhaps redundant, but the thrust is simply that relitigation cannot be had, as illustrated by Commonwealth of Pennsylvania v. Bierly,[550] where a person who secured a land patent from the state on an application which either mistakely or falsely alleged that the land was vacant, cannot claim that the state is estopped by reason of the land patent that it issued from establishing prior, paramount title in the state, as there was an estoppel against estoppel. Indeed, an estoppel may be set up against another estoppel with the result that the estoppel is neutralized or destroyed.[551] If both parties claim under the same person and one is estopped by one deed and the other is estopped by another deed, both deeds made by that person, one estoppel offsets the other estoppel.[552]

10.5 ELECTION OF REMEDIES

At early common law there was no preclusive doctrine of res judicata, and unless barred by a statute of limitation a plaintiff could sue under one writ and if unsuccessful sue subsequently under a different writ. By the middle of the eighteenth century the English courts had so expanded the scope of many writs that there were large areas of overlapping, and the litigious society reveled in promiscuous litigation. To meet this problem the common law courts fashioned the doctrine of election of remedies: a plaintiff who chose a writ on which he could recover was deemed to have "elected" his remedy and was precluded from using another writ in a subsequent suit. In the United States in the nineteenth century the election of remedies doctrine was intended to include equitable remedies, and a plaintiff who had available to him a remedy at law and a remedy in equity had to "elect" his remedy to the exclusion of the other remedy. Thus, a plaintiff who "elected" a remedy which he could not obtain for some reason or other was in some jurisdictions precluded by his election of remedies from pursuing subsequently the other remedy. Even where law and equity remained separate a plaintiff could not assert his two potential remedies in the same suit, so that the statute of limitations would ordinarily have run by the time the plaintiff had been authoritatively advised that his election of remedies was erroneous.[553]

Today these results are avoided because a plaintiff can seek remedies in the alternative and have both remedies in the same suit. However, in Carter v. Superior Court[554] an employee, intentionally injured by his employer and thus having the option of claiming workman's compensation or suing the employer for civil damages, was precluded by the California court from seeking the latter remedy by successfully prosecuting his claim for worker's compensation.

10.6 COMPULSORY COUNTERCLAIM

Another form of preclusion is the compulsory counterclaim rule that is invoked in a suit subsequent to that in which compliance with the rule was required. Probably the first general compulsory counterclaim rule was adopted in California in the 1872 revision of Section 439 of the California Code of Civil Procedure; later in 1912 Rule 13 of the Federal Rules of Civil Procedure (formerly Rule 30 of the Federal Equity Rules) required a defendant to assert as counterclaim any claim he has arising out of the transaction sued upon in the first suit, hence the compulsory counterclaim. While the sanction for failure to assert a compulsory counterclaim is not provided today in Rule 13 (a) of the Federal Rules of Civil Procedure, the general view is that an action may not thereafter be brought on the counterclaim.[555]

It is self-evident that a defendant must interpose in the first suit all defenses he has to that claim; if he omits to put in a defense, or the defense is ruled on adversely to his interests, the defendant cannot thereafter use the counterclaim in any way to attack or defeat the operation of the judgment, unless the defense itself is part of a collateral or even direct attack on the judgment itself.[556] Nevertheless, there may be situations where the result is difficult, as where the defendant has grounds for claiming affirmative relief in his favor, to wit: (1) there is no substantial factual nexus between plaintiff's claim and defendant's counterclaim; (2) the claim and counterclaim arise out of the same transaction and the forum rule mandates a compulsory counterclaim; and (3) the claim and counterclaim have a factual nexus and arise out of the same transaction but the forum rule does not mandate a compulsory counterclaim. In the first situation, the defendant is not compelled to assert his counterclaim in the initial suit, and the defendant runs no risk that he will be later precluded, because the factual issues in the two suits are distinct and different; indeed, the defendant may assert his counterclaim in the initial action or assert it subsequently in a separate suit. In the second situation, the defendant must assert his counterclaim because of the forum rule in favor of compulsory counterclaim; should defendant fail to assert his defense, he is precluded from doing so in a later suit.[557] In the third situation, where there is no compulsory counterclaim rule in the forum, the defendant, from a pragmatic position, must assert his counterclaim in the first suit because (a) under the rule of issue preclusion he will be prevented from relitigating any issues determined against him in the adjudication of plaintiff's claim in the first suit;[558] and (b) the defendant may not in a subsequent suit assert a counterclaim which would nullify or undermine a judgment that plaintiff recovered in the first suit.[559] Should the defendant decide to withhold his counterclaim in the first action, for whatever reason, he may be subsequently precluded from doing so by the rule against "splitting" a cause of action.[560]

Where the forum rendering the judgment in the first suit has a compulsory counterclaim rule and the forum entertaining the subsequent suit does not have a compulsory counterclaim rule, the forum in the first suit will generally hold sway, as delineated in Sections 94 and 95 of Restatement (Second) of Conflict of Laws.[561]

Where the first suit is settled before trial, the issue of the counterclaim in the subsequent suit will generally be decided against the defendant should he endeavor to raise the counterclaim in the subsequent action. In Datta v. Staab[562] the plaintiff S in an automobile collision sued D, whose defense was assumed by his liability insurance company; D then hired his own attorney to sue S for personal injuries in a subsequent action, S's defense being assumed by S's insurance company. S's insurer in the subsequent action raised the defense that D's claim was a counterclaim that should have been asserted in the first suit by S against D, which suit had been settled by D's insurer. The California appellate court agreed and dismissed D's subsequent suit against S for D's failure to assert the counterclaim in the first suit by S against D.

In short, tactical considerations usually dictate that a defendant will assert his counterclaim in the first suit rather than run any risk of preclusion in the subsequent suit.

An insurance carrier making payments to the mortgagee is normally subrogated to the rights of the mortgagee, and normally would include a counterclaim (for reimbursement of monies paid to the mortgagee) against the insured. In Smith v. Insurance Company of North America[563] the federal court in Tennessee allowed the defendant insurer to counterclaim against the insured's estate on a subrogation theory, even though no money had actually been paid to the mortgagee. And in Cerullo v. Aetna Casualty & Surety Co.[564] the New York court held that the defendant insurer should be allowed to amend its answer to allege a counterclaim based on subrogation to the mortgagee's interest and fraudulent conduct by the insured. The counterclaim here is compulsory, especially where the issues of fact and law raised by the claim and counterclaim are largely the same;[565] where res judicata would bar a subsequent suit on a defendant's claim absent the compulsory counterclaim rule;[566] where substantially the same evidence supports or refutes plaintiff's claim as well as defendant's counterclaim;[567] and where there is a logical relationship between the claim and the counterclaim.[568] The subrogation claim that would arise from the same transaction or occurrence as the insured's action against the insurer would likely satisfy the requirements of a compulsory counterclaim, or vice versa. One exception is that a party need not assert a claim which at the time of serving his pleading has not matured.[569] A party who chooses not to assert a mature claim, on the other hand, runs a risk that his subsequent claim will be dismissed for failure to assert a counterclaim in the prior pending action. But there is a still a risk, as illustrated by Payne v. Buffalo Reinsurance Co.,[570] where plaintiffs, who purchased a factory by giving a note and deed of trust to the seller, insured the factory against fire with the defendant. When fire destroyed the factory, the defendant insurer paid the seller-mortgagee and took an assignment of the note and deed of trust; the insurer denied liability to the plaintiffs. Plaintiffs then sued to recover under the fire insurance policy, and defendant counterclaimed as subrogee of the mortgagee for the amount paid on the mortgage. Summary judgment was given in favor of the defendant. The plaintiffs later sued to cancel the deed of trust held by the defendant insurer, and the North Carolina trial court ruled in plaintiff's favor, finding that the defendant had made a binding election by counterclaiming in the earlier suit.

The North Carolina Court of Appeals affirmed to the effect that the insurer was precluded from further action on the mortgage:

Since the rights and remedies are quite different, and defendant actively and formally pursued its subrogation rights in the previous litigation between the parties by seeking to obtain a money judgment on that ground, and chose not to assert its right under the mortgage, those rights cannot be successfully asserted now in this action. They had been abandoned under the terms of the policy. . . .

Thus, the insurer may not both counterclaim as a subrogee and foreclose on the mortgage.

10.7 STAY OF PROCEEDINGS

Still another preclusive device centers about the stay of proceedings, as illustrated by Cohan v. United Benefit Life Insurance Co.[571] Here the Ohio plaintiff beneficiary of a life insurance policy on the life of her father sued the insurance carrier in Ohio for $5,000, the face amount of the policy. Two months later the insurer filed an action in interpleader in a California court and asked for a preliminary injunction to restrain plaintiff from proceeding with her Ohio suit. The Ohio lower court then responded:

On consideration of the pleadings, affidavits, and exhibits, the court finds that it has prior jurisdiction of the within matter and that it would be oppressive to the plaintiff to be restrained by another court from proceeding with the within action, and accordingly, It Is Hereby Ordered, Adjudged, and Decreed that the defendant be and hereby is enjoined from in any manner assisting, aiding, participating or engaging directly or indirectly in the prosecution or conduct of the action now pending in [the California court]. . . .

The Ohio Court of Appeals, however, favored the California suit, and in particular the procedure of interpleader, which "has been recognized as proper under the circumstances over the centuries. It is designed to protect a stakeholder when there are conflicting claims against the funds which are admittedly due to some one but the proper one is not known and a court of competent jurisdiction is asked to legally adjudicate the conflict."[572] Furthermore, according to the Ohio appellate court, "it is apparent that the Cuyahoga County [Ohio] court cannot obtain jurisdiction over the person of the other claimant since she is a resident of California." The Ohio appellate court concluded:

We know of no reason why the merits of this action cannot be resolved by the California court where a final and complete adjudication of this matter can be had. We likewise cannot agree with the conclusion reached by the [Ohio] trial court that it would be oppressive to plaintiff to be restrained by another court from proceeding with the within action. While we agree that a court has a duty and power to protect its jurisdiction, we are of the opinion that the court seeking to do so should not overlook its inability to do complete and final justice where such fact becomes apparent to the court.

Thus, the preclusive device of stay of proceedings rests on the determination that there is a pending action between the same parties concerning the same subject matter. However, the ''plea in abatement'' results in the dismissal of the second action;[573] the stay of proceedings simply suspends prosecution of the second action until the first action is properly terminated. The motion to stay may be granted where the prior action involves closely related issues, even though it is not clear that res judicata will result.[574] ''Parallel filing'' in disregard of the compulsory counterclaim rule[575] often gives rise to the need of a stay of proceedings.[576] The ''plea in abatement'' to dismiss the second action also finds prominence in the ''parallel filing'' situation, and will be sustained when it appears that the first action, were it to go to judgment, would be res judicata of the second action.[577]

10.8 JUDGMENT ON THE MERITS

A judgment on the merits is preclusive where the judgment was grounded upon plaintiff's failure to state a valid cause of action. But where the subsequent action is based on a complaint that has been reformulated so as to state a valid cause of action, or where defendant was granted a nonsuit after plaintiff's presentation of evidence at trial, many legal scholars argue that the subsequent suit is not precluded.[578] In Commissioner of Internal Revenue v. Sunnen[579] the taxpayer obtained a determination that certain income in a particular tax year was not attributable to him; subsequently the identical question arose in a suit against another taxpayer, but the federal government won the case. The highest court ruled that the first judgment on the merits cannot estop the federal government, or otherwise the first taxpayer will have a perennial special tax exemption not available to any other taxpayer!

Judgment on the merts normally should be preclusive and result in a merger or bar.

10.9 SUBSTANTIVE RELATIONSHIP

Substantive legal relationship often results in preclusion, as shown in such categories as family, contract and property, organizational affiliation, and indemnitor and indemnitee. Where a husband sues for his own injuries and loses the action, the judgment against him may preclude the wife from suing for her loss of consortium or loss of support, resulting from her husband's injury.[580] However, that judgment ordinarily would not preclude the wife from suing for her own personal injuries suffered in the same accident with her husband,[581] because her claim for personal injuries is independent of her husband's claim for his personal injuries, while her claim for loss of consortium or loss of support is said to be derivative of his claim, and is therefore precluded when the husband lost his suit. Indeed, a losing suit for medical expenses can preclude a later suit for medical expenses in a personal injury suit by another member of the family.[582] Issue preclusion also applies where a family member who was physically injured loses his action to recover for his personal injuries and every family member is bound by that determination in a subsequent action for loss of companionship, for example.[583]

Under contract and property substantive relationship the issue preclusion is also observable: a contract may be enforced by either the promisee or the third party beneficiary, and a judgment against the beneficiary, for example, will preclude the promisee from enforcing the contract in his own behalf; a judgment for or against the promisee precludes an action by the third party beneficiary if, under the law of contracts, the promisee had the power at the time the judgment was rendered to discharge the promisor.[584] In the property substantive relationship a judgment affecting one owner of the property will have ordinarily no effect against the other property owner, unless that other property owner is actually made a party to the litigation in which even he may be bound by the litigation.[585] Res judicata is generally applicable to both community property and to bailments, although today it is held that the spouse or co-owner of the property under community property will not be bound by an adverse judgment against the other spouse unless both owners are made parties to the action.[586] In the bailment situation a judgment for or against the bailor or bailee in an action asserting a claim for loss or damage to the bailed property precludes either bailor or bailee from subsequently suing for the loss.[587]

Organizational relationships mean that members are bound by judgments for or against the organization, whether it be a corporation, a partnership, or any other entity of organized persons. Indeed, in the absence of collusion, a judgment to which the corporation is a party, for example, is conclusive upon the stockholders, so that the stockholders may not via a stockholder's derivative action seek to relitigate the matters that were adjudicated.[588]

The indemnitor-indemnitee substantive relationship also gives rise to preclusion, i.e., where one person (the indemnitee) who has been held liable to an injured party, for example, is entitled to be recompensed for his liability by payment from another (the indemnitor). The most common indemnity relationship is that between the insured and his insurer, and the claim by the injured person against the insured or indemnitee may very well preclude a claim by the indemnitee against the insurer or indemnitor. Of course, the indemnitee calls upon the indemnitor to defend the former's interest in the first lawsuit, and the resulting judgment binds both the indemnitee and the indemnitor in the ordinary situation. The indemnitor generally is estopped to dispute the resulting judgment once that judgment has been fairly determined.

10.10 TOTAL RES JUDICATA

The concept of "total res judicata" was echoed by Justice Traynor of the California Supreme Court in Keidatz v. Albany,[589] which action dealt with damages for fraud; plaintiffs alleged that they were induced to buy a newly constructed home from the defendants by certain false and fraudulent representations respecting the character of the construction and its location on the particular land. Defendants contended that the action was barred by two previous adjudications between the parties, to wit: plaintiff's action to rescind the contract for fraud and failure of consideration was defeated by demurrer, and a demurrer to the second amended complaint was also sustained and judgment was entered for the defendants for costs. Defendants claimed "total res judicata"barring the present suit, and also pointed out that "a party claiming to have been defrauded must seek all relief to which he may be entitled in one action, and . . . he may not, after having failed in an action to rescind a contract for fraud, thereafter bring a second action for damages." But Justice Traynor did not accept defendants' argument:

> It has been the settled rule in this state that a judgment entered on a demurrer does not have such broad res judicata effect. . . . Less prejudice is suffered by a defendant who has had only to attack the pleadings, than by one who has been forced to go to trial . . . and the hardship suffered by being forced to defend against a new action, instead of against an amended complaint, is not materially greater. . . . We do not feel, however, that at this time we should reweigh the conflicting arguments over the wisdom of the rule we apply.[590]

Total res judicata was applicable in Hinchley v. Sellers,[591] where the New York Court of Appeals ascribed preclusive effect to an earlier New Hampshire judgment in which the plaintiffs lost on the ground that the defendant's automobile at the time of the accident was driven without the "permission" of the named insured. (Pennsylvania law governed the insurance policy and the meaning of "permission.") In the subsequent wrongful death action against the owners of the automobile in New York the question was whether the defendants were liable under Section 59 of the New York Vehicle and Traffic Law, an issue which turned upon whether one O'Rourke had driven the automobile with "permission" of the named insured under the New York statute. The highest New York court opined:

> It was found as the fact in the New Hampshire action that "the limitation upon the permission given in this case was that the car should not be used at all if O'Rourke was a passenger." This was not a fragmentary finding of an evidentiary fact . . . but was a finding essential to the judgment, from which the resolution of the ultimate legal issue necessarily followed. It is perfectly clear from the record of the New Hampshire proceedings that the quoted factual finding was a necessary step in arriving at the final judgment. . . .

Notes

1. Currie, "Mutuality of Collateral Estoppel: Limits of the Bernhard Doctrine," 9 Stan L Rev 281 (1957) at p. 289.

2. See 31 ALR3d 1044 (1970).

3. See 30A Am Jur Judgments 324 (1958). See generally 12 Capital Univ L Rev 681 (1983).

4. See Siegel New York Practice 442–443 (1978); also generally 45 Albany L Rev (1981) at pp. 1032 et seq.

5. See Winters v. Lavine, 574 F2d 46 (2nd Cir., 1978), for example.

6. Note the 1837 English decision of Pickard v. Sears, 6 Ad & El 469, 112 Eng Rep 179 (1837), where English Lord Coke classified and illustrated estoppels as follows:

> Touching estoppels, which is an excellent and curious kinde of learning, it is to be observed, that there be three kinde of estoppels, viz. by matter of record, by matter in writing, and by matter *in paiis*. (a) By matter of record, viz. by letter patents, fine, recoverie, pleading, taking of continuance, confession, imparlance, warrant of atturney, admittance. (b) by matter in writing, as by deed indented, by making of an acquittance by deed indented or deed poll, (c) . . . by matter *in paiis*, as by liverie, by entry, by acceptance of rent, by partition, and by acceptance of an estate, as here in the case that *Littleton* putteth; whereof *Littleton* maketh a speciall observation, that a man shall be estopped by matter in the countrey, without any writing. [2 Coke's First Institutes (1817), Section 352a]

7. See Commercial National Bank v. Nacogdoches Compress & Warehouse Co., 133 F 501 (5th Cir., 1904).

8. See Furst & Thomas v. Smith, 133 SW2d 941 (Ky., 1939).

9. See Sections 872 and 894 (1) of Restatement (Second) of Torts.

10. See Section 894 (2) of Restatement (Second) of Torts.

11. See United States v. Head, 697 F2d 1200 (4th Cir., 1982), cert den 103 S Ct 3113 (1983).

12. See Moore v. United States, 360 F2d 353 (4th Cir., 1965).

13. See Hooper v. Guthrie, 390 F Supp 1327 (WD Pa., 1975); see generally 33 Am Univ L Rev 643 (1984).

14. See Evergreens v. Nunan, 141 F2d 927 (2nd Cir., 1944), cert den 323 US 720 (1944).

15. 456 US 461 (1982).

16. Supra notes 9 and 10.

17. 440 US 147 (1979).

18. 716 F2d 1455 (5th Cir., 1983).

19. 493 NYS2d 829 (1985).

20. Id.

> . . . This record reveals new evidence, not available at the time of the prior proceeding, which could certainly have changed the prior result. . . . The record also clearly reveals that [Kutcher's] counsel in the prior litigation failed to actually litigate any issues relating to strict product liability for a design defect, apparently due to an understandable confusion regarding the subtle distinctions between a cause of action sounding in negligent design (for which recovery may be had only by direct suit against the tortfeasor) and a cause of action sounding in strict product liability for a design defect (as to which a recovery may be had from the vendor as well as the manufacturer). . . . It has been observed that these two theories of liability "are, in New York, almost functionally equivalent." . . . On these particular facts, we are not persuaded that it would be fair to preclude [Kutcher's] from litigating the issue of whether the machine in question was manufactured with a design defect.

21. 65 NY2d 449, 482 NE2d 63 (1985).

22. See 35 West 43rd Street Realty Corp. v. Bieber, decided May 2, 1986, by the New York Supreme Court, New York County:

> The doctrine of *res judicata* is designed to provide finality in the resolution of disputes, and bars relitigation between the same parties, or their privies, where a prior action has resulted in a judgment on the merits of the same cause of action (Reilly v. Reid, 45 NY2d 24). Once a claim or cause of action is finally adjudicated, all other claims arising from the same series of transactions are barred, whether based on different theories or seeking different remedies (O'Brien v. City of Syracuse, 54 NY2d 353; Reilly v. Reid, supra, 45 NY2d 24). In determining whether a judgment should be given *res judicata* effect, the court must determine whether a different judgment in the second action would obliterate or impair the rights and interests created by the first, whether the same evidence is required to support both claims, and whether there is an identity of essential factual matter in both lawsuits (see Tucker v. Arthur Anderson & Co., 646 F2d 721, 2nd Cir., 1981).

23. ——NYS2d——(1986).

24. See 52 Miss L J (1982) at pp. 766 et seq.

25. Note Parklane Hosiery Co. v. Shore, 439 US 322 (1979), delineated at length herein at Chapter 5.

26. See National Tea Co. v. Confection Specialties, Inc., 362 NE2d 1150 (Ill., 1977).

27. See Freeman v. Marine Midland Bank, 419 F Supp 440 (EDNY, 1976).

28. See Boucher v. Bailey, 375 A2d 1160 (N.H., 1977). See generally 15 New Eng L Rev (1979) at pp. 5 et seq.

29. Note Expert Electric, Inc. v. Levine, 554 F2d 1227 (2nd Cir., 1977) cert den 434 US 903 (1977).

30. See Pilla v. Alexander, 558 F2d 509 (8th Cir., 1977), cert den 434 US 971 (1977).

31. See 85 La L Rev 158 (1974) and 44 St John's L Rev 165 (1969).

32. See Perrotta v. Irizarry, 430 F Supp 1274 (SDNY, 1977), aff 573 F2d 1294 (2nd Cir., 1977).

33. See Kyreacos v. Smith, 572 P2d 723 (Wash., 1977).

34. See Miller v. Poretsky, 409 F Supp 837 (DC Cir., 1976).

35. See Buckland, Text-Book of Roman Law (1921), at pp. 690–692.

36. See 35 Ill L Rev 41 (1940).

37. Id. at pp. 44, 51, 53, 58–59.

38. 109 Eng Rep 1177 (KB, 1831).

39. For a historical perspective, see Robertson v. Robertson, 61 So2d 499 (Fla., 1952) at p. 502.

40. 94 US 351 (1877).

41. 78 US 139 (1870).

42. Supra note 40 at pp. 352–353.

43. Supra note 40.

44. Supra note 40.

45. Supra note 40 at p. 359.

46. 19 Cal2d 807, 122 P2d 892 (1942).

47. Id. at pp. 813 and 895.

48. 202 US 281 (1906).

49. 285 US 22 (1932).

50. 33 USC 901–950.

51. 310 US 381 (1940).

52. 384 US 394 (1966).

53. Note 46 Geo L Rev 65 (1977).

54. 439 US 322 (1979). Also note 32 Stan L Rev 655 (1980).

55. Id. at pp. 332–333.

56. See Section 27 of Restatement (Second) of Judgments.

57. 440 US 147 (1979).

58. 449 US 90 (1980).

59. See commentary in note 53.

60. See White, Patterns of American Legal Thought (1978), at pp. 101–102, 166–172; also 36 Harv L Rev 802 (1923).

61. See 66 Mich L Rev 1723 (1968) and 44 S Cal L Rev 1036 (1971).

62. Note 45 U Chi L Rev 317 (1978), 70 Northwestern U L Rev 859 (1976), and 91 Harv L Rev 1281 (1978).

63. 206 US 285 (1907).

64. Id. at pp. 288–289.

65. See Robbins v. District Court, 592 F2d 1015 (8th Cir., 1979), cert den 100 S Ct 107 (1979).

66. 1B Moore's Federal Practice Section 0.411 (1974). See generally 4 Am J Trial Adv 75 (1980).

67. 3 T. Ireland, Coke's Abridgement 274–275 (1813).

68. See Vestal, Res Judicata/Preclusion V5–V6 (1969).

69. See Montana v. United States, 440 US 147 (1979) at pp. 153–154.

70. Lawlor v. National Screen Service, 349 US 322 (1955) at p. 326.

71. See State v. Stauffer, 536 P2d 1044 (Ariz., 1975), and Murphy v. Richford, 371 NE2d 260 (Ill., 1977).

72. See Expert Electric, Inc. v. Levine, supra note 29, holding that the privity requisite prevents a litigant from being bound by a prior judgment where he had no notice of the claim asserted therein and had no opportunity to present his argument in the case.

73. See 11 Tulsa L J 305 (1976) at p. 327.

74. 57 Cal App3d 341 (1985).

75. 453 A2d 1285 (N.H., 1985).

76. See generally 44 Tenn L Rev 927 (1977) and 45 Ind L J 1 (1969).

77. See Katz v. Eli Lilly & Co., 84 FRD 378 (EDNY, 1979), where jurors were deposed in the prior action to determine if the verdict represented compromise.

78. See Bahler v. Fletcher, 474 P2d 329 (Ore., 1960), where the court characterized the inadequacy of the attorney. Also 52 Miss L J (1982) at pp. 776 et seq.

79. See United States v. United Air Lines, Inc., 216 F Supp 709 (D Nev., 1962).

80. See Spettigue v. Mahoney, 445 P2d 557 (Ariz., 1968):

> The selection of the judge and jury, the choice of counsel, the availability of witnesses, the manner of presentation of their testimony, the dynamics of the rapport between witnesses and fact-finder, and the personalities and appearances of the parties as they impress the fact-finder in various ways, are all matters that defy scientific analysis, are affected by fortuitous circumstances and variously determine the outcome of a contest conducted in the courts of this country.

81. 378 F2d 876 (5th Cir., 1967), cert den 389 US 1009 (1967).

82. Supra note 70.

83. Subparagraph 7 thereof.

84. Subparagraph 15 thereof.

85. 380 F2d 69 (4th Cir., 1967), cert den 389 US 1004 (1967), reh den 389 US 1059 (1967).

86. See 68 Columbia L Rev 1457 (1968) at p. 1461.

87. Supra note 46.

88. See Chapter 4 herein at Section 4.1 thereof.

89. 402 US 313 (1971).

90. See generally 31 AL R3d 1044 at p. 1052.

91. Supra note 79.

92. 24 NY2d 65, 246 NE2d 725 (1969).

93. 386 F Supp 934 (D Pa., 1985).

94. See 1982 Ariz St L J 45 (1982) at p. 50.

95. 157 NW 723 (Minn., 1916).

96. Cromwell v. County of Sac, 94 US 351 (1876).

97. Supra note 94 at p. 51.

98. See generally 16 U Rich L Rev 341 (1984) at p. 344.

99. ——Md——(1986).

100. 250 NY 304, 165 NE 456 (1929).

101. Supra note 96.

102. See 31 Hast L J 755 (1980) at pp. 763–764.

103. 442 US 127 (1979).

104. 60 B.R. 621, 14 B.C.D. 530 (Bankr SDNY, 1986).

105. Supra note 54.

106. See 13 Ind L Rev 563 (1980) generally.

107. Id.

108. Cf. Teitelbaum Furs, Inc. v. Dominion Insurance Co., 375 P2d 439 (Cal., 1962).

109. See Berner v. British Commonwealth Pacific Airlines, Ltd., 346 F2d 532 (2nd Cir., 1965).

110. Id.

111. Supra note 109.

112. Supra note 54.

113. Supra note 54 at p. 332.

114. Supra note 109.

115. 216 F Supp 709 (ED Wash., 1962).

116. Id. at p. 730.

117. Supra note 106.

118. 141 F2d 927 (2nd Cir., 1944).

119. Id. at p. 929.

120. 327 F2d 944 (2nd Cir., 1964).

121. 479 NY2d 163, 468 NE2d 1 (1984). Suit was brought by the City of New York and fourteen "public benefit corporations" including the Transit Authority and the Health and Hospitals Corporation. The ad damnum was $45 million, but the New York Court of Appeals invalidated about half that amount; other damage claims against the utility exceeded $160 million.

122. Food Pageant v. Consolidated Edison Co., 54 NY2d 167 (1981), where a jury awarded the plaintiff grocery chain the sum of $40,500 in damages for food spoilage caused by the utility's gross negligence.

123. The Court of Appeals' decision means that New York City and its agencies may proceed with that portion of their suit which seeks damages for personal injuries and property damage resulting from service interruptions, as well as damage caused by looting and vandalism: "Plaintiffs have shown facts sufficient to require a trial of the factual question of whether intervention of the rioters was within the contemplation of the parties or reasonably to have been foreseen by Con Edison," Judge Hugh R. Jones wrote for the court. See NYLJ, July 2, 1984, p. 8.

124. 50 AD2d 211, 377 NYS2d 118 (1975).

125. Judge Shapiro in reversing a verdict for the plaintiff and ordering a new trial opined:

> The doctrine of collateral estoppel stems from the doctrine of res judicata, at the core of which is the idea that society's interests are better served by foreclosing repetitious litigation than by permitting litigants to show that the truth is otherwise than as found or assumed in a prior action. Collateral estoppel falls into the category of partial res judicata because its binding effect is limited to certain of the issues formerly in dispute, rather than extending to the entire controversy. When collateral estoppel operates, certain questions actually litigated and determined in one action are precluded from relitigation in a later action when the questions arise anew, even in a suit on a different cause of action.

126. See DES Litigation Reporter (July 12, 1982) at p. 1695.

127. 232 A2d 470 (N.J., 1967).

128. Id. at p. 475.

129. Supra note 54 at p. 330.

130. Supra note 106.

131. See Gramatan Home Investors Corp. v. Lopez, 46 NY2d 481, 386 NE2d 1328 (1979) at pp. 481 and 1331, respectively.

132. 94 US 351 (1876) at pp. 352–353.
133. See Chapter 3 herein.
134. 102 Eng Rep 630 (1803).
135. Id. at p. 633.
136. See 35 Ill L Rev 41 (1940) at p. 52.
137. Id. at p. 53.
138. See generally 41 Missouri L Rev 521 (1976).
139. See Section 4.1 herein.
140. See generally 120 U of Penna L Rev 147 (1981).
141. See Flynn v. State Board of Chiropractic Examiners, 418 F2d 668 (9th Cir., 1969).
142. According to Adamson v. Hill, 449 P2d 536 (Kan., 1969), the courts are more inclined to permit use of collateral estoppel as a "shield" (i.e., defensively) rather than as a "sword" (i.e., offensively).
143. See Chapter 5 herein.
144. See 35 Tulane L Rev 301 (1961).
145. Bruszewski v. United States, 181 F2d 419 (3rd Cir., 1950) at p. 423, cert den 340 US 865 (1950).
146. 1B Moore's Federal Practice § 0.411 (1) at p. 1255 (1974).
147. 68 Columbia L Rev 1457 (1968) at p. 1461.
148. See, for example, Kuehn v. Garcia, 608 F2d 1143 (8th Cir., 1979); Darin & Armstrong, Inc. v. Ben Agree Co., 276 NW2d 869 (Mich., 1979); and Gilmer v. Porterfield, 212 SE2d 842 (Ga., 1975).
149. Bernhard v. Bank of America, 122 P2d 892 (Cal., 1942).
150. 402 US 313 (1971).
151. 443 NE2d 978 (Ohio, 1983).
152. 381 F Supp 926 (SD Fla., 1974).
153. Supra note 151 at p. 987.
154. Supra note 151 at p. 984.
155. See 12 Capital U L Rev 681 (1983) at p. 685.
156. Supra note 54 at p. 331.
157. Comment to Section 88:

> A person in such a position that he might *ordinarily* have been expected to join as plaintiff in the first action, but who did not do so, may be refused the benefits of "offensive" issue preclusion where the circumstances suggest that he wished to avail himself of the benefits of a favorable outcome without incurring the risk of an unfavorable one. Such a refusal may be appropriate where the person could *reasonably* have been expected to intervene in the prior action, and ordinarily is appropriate where he withdrew from an action to which he had been a party.

158. 327 F2d 944 (2nd Cir., 1964), cert den 377 US 934 (1964).
159. 191 NE2d 771 (Mass., 1963).
160. 453 A2d 1278 (N.H., 1982).
161. 441 F Supp 62 (D Mo., 1977).
162. 494 F2d 1104 (DC Cir., 1974).
163. Id. at p. 1115.
164. 24 NY2d 65, 246 NE2d 725 (1969).
165. Supra note 150.
166. Supra note 150 at p. 330.
167. See MPC, Inc. v. Kenny, 367 A2d 486 (Md., 1977).

168. 6A Moore's Federal Practice § 60.02 (1979).

169. Cromwell v. County of Sac, 94 US 351 (1977) at pp. 352–353.

170. 681 F2d 334 (5th Cir., 1982).

171. 493 F2d 1076 (5th Cir., 1974).

172. See Parklane Hosiery Co. v. Shore, 439 US 322 (1979).

173. Note Ezagui v. Dow Chemical Co., 598 F2d 727 (2nd Cir., 1979), on the question of new evidence, and Katz v. Eli Lilly & Co., 84 FRD 378 (EDNY, 1979), on issue of compromise verdict.

174. Rust v. First National Bank, 466 F Supp 135 (D Wyo., 1985).

175. See Mackris v. Murray, 397 F2d 74 (6th Cir., 1968), where a justice of the peace heard the initial suit.

176. 408 P2d 849 (Ariz., 1965).

177. Id. at p. 852.

178. See Rachal v. Hill, 435 F2d 59 (5th Cir., 1970) at p. 62, cert den 403 US 904 (1971).

179. See Blumcraft of Pittsburgh v. Kawneer Co., 482 F2d 542 (5th Cir., 1973), rejecting the argument that prior inconsistent decisions preclude application of collateral estoppel.

180. See Travelers Insurance Co. v. Thompson, 163 NW2d 289 (Minn., 1974).

181. See United States v. Standefer, 610 F2d 1076 (3rd Cir., 1979).

182. See generally 39 Iowa L Rev 217 (1954).

183. Supra note 54.

184. 281 F2d.

185. Id. at p. 346.

186. Nevarov v. Caldwell, 327 P2d 111 (Cal App., 1958).

187. Id., at p. 119.

188. Supra note 149.

189. 232 A2d 470 (N.J., 1967).

190. 4 FRD 378 (1979).

191. 497 NYS2d 58, 114AD2d 46; app dism'd 68 NY2d 753, 497 NE2d 709 (1985).

192. Id.

193. See Fairchild, Arabatzis & Smith, Inc. v. Prometer Co., Ltd., 470 F Supp 610 (SDNY, 1979).

194. See Flora Maritima Browning de Cuba v. M/V Ciudad de la Habana, 218 F Supp 938 (D Md., 1963).

195. See Kane v. Central American Mining & Oil Inc., 235 F Supp 559 (SDNY, 1964).

196. See Bata v. Bata, 163 A2d 493 (Del., 1960), cert den 366 US 964 (1961).

197. 191 So 94 (Miss., 1939), aff 195 So 322 (1940).

198. For a critical view see 24 Ohio St L J 381 (1963): "[W]here the plaintiff chooses to commence a quasi-in-rem action in a jurisdiction which recognizes the defendant's right to make a limited appearance . . . he should not be permitted to negate the limitation by a later suit for the deficiency in a jurisdiction not recognizing the limited appearance in its own courts."

199. See Hodgson v. Royal Crown Bottling Co., 465 F2d 473 (5th Cir., 1972).

200. See Commissioner of Internal Revenue v. Sunnen, 333 US 591 (1948).

201. See Parke Davis & Co. v. Stromsodt, 441 F2d 1390 (8th, 1969), and Young v. United States, 518 F Supp 921 (SDNY, 1981).

202. 681 F2d 334 (5th Cir., 1982).

203. 541 F Supp 1384 (ED Pa., 1982).
204. 26 A 324 (N.J., 1893).
205. Id. at p. 327.
206. 333 A2d 728 (Pa., 1985).
207. 439 US 322 (1978).
208. See 16 U Rich L Rev 341 (1982) generally.
209. See Section 4.1 of Chapter 4 herein.
210. See 41 Missouri L Rev 521 (1976).
211. See Bigelow v. Old Dominion Copper Mining & Smelting Co., 225 US 111 (1912) at p. 126.
212. Supra note 54.
213. 599 F2d 274 (8th Cir., 1979).
214. See Montana v. United States, 440 US 147 (1979) at p. 153.
215. Supra note 54.
216. Id. at p. 330.
217. See Berner v. British Commonwealth Pacific Airlines Ltd., 346 F2d 532 (2nd Cir., 1965), cert den 382 US 983 (1966).
218. 15 USC 78j (b), 78n (a), and 78t (a). See generally 5 U of Dayton L Rev 1 (1980) at pp. 208 et seq.
219. Securities & Exchange Commission v. Parklane Hosiery Co., Inc., 558 F2d 1083 (2nd Cir., 1977).
220. 565 F2d 815 (2nd Cir., 1977).
221. See Section 4.4 of Chapter 4 herein.
222. Supra note 54.
223. 15 USC 78u (g).
224. 319 US 372 (1962).
225. Id.
226. 359 US 510 (1964).
227. 430 US 442 (1977).
228. Id. at p. 450. See generally 57 Minn L Rev 639 (1973).
229. 550 P2d 1185 (Ore., 1976).
230. Pacific Northwestern Bell Telephone Co. v. Century Home Components, Inc., 514 P2d 871 (Ore., 1973).
231. See Sylvester v. Century Home Components, Inc., and Hesse v. Century Home Components, Inc., 514 P2d 871 (Ore., 1973).
232. See generally 1982 Ariz St L J 45 (1982).
233. 485 F Supp 242 (ED Tex., 1980).
234. 493 F2d 1076 (5th Cir., 1973), cert den 419 US 896 (1974).
235. Supra note 233 at p. 247.
236. Supra note 233 at p. 248.
237. See McCarty v. Johns-Manville Sales Corp., 502 F Supp 335 (SD Miss., 1980).
238. Id. at p. 339.
239. See Tretter v. Johns-Manville Corp., 88 FRD 329 (1980).
240. 18 USC 1961[–]1968.
241. 471 P2d 370 (Alas., 1970).
242. See generally 4 Am J of Trial Adv 75 (1980).
243. 445 P2d 557 (Ariz., 1968).
244. See 16 Rich L Rev 341 (1982) at p. 353.

245. 247 A2d 185 (N.H., 1968).

246. 451 P2d 814 (Haw., 1971).

247. 397 F2d 185 (5th Cir., 1968).

248. Arthur v. Evangelical Deaconess Society, 615 SW2d 438 (Mo App., 1981). States permitting the offensive assertion of collateral estoppel include: CALIFORNIA: R. B. Spriggs Co., Inc. v. Adolph Coors Co., 94 Cal. App. 3d 419, 156 Cal. Rptr. 738, 743–745 (1979); COLORADO: Waitkus v. Pomeroy, 183 Colo. 344, 517 P.2d 396, 400 (1973); DELAWARE: Foltz v. Pullman, Inc., 319 A.2d 38 (Del. Super. Ct. 1974); In Re TransOcean Tender Offer Securities Litigation, 455 F. Supp. 999, 1005 (N.D. Ill., 1978) (interpreting Delaware law); MAINE: Hossler v. Barry, 403 A.2d 762, 769 (Me., 1979); MARYLAND: Maryland v. Capital Airlines, Inc., 267 F. Supp. 298 (D. Md., 1967); Gielblum v. Bloom, 21 Md. App. 406, 319 A.2d 546 (Ct. Spec. App., 1974); MINNESOTA: Pacific Indemnity Co. v. Thompson-Yaeger, Inc., 260 N.W. 2d 548, 550 (Minn., 1977); Lustrik v. Rankila, 269 Minn. 515, 131 N.W. 2d 741 (1964); NEVADA: United States v. United Air Lines, Inc., 216 F. Supp. 709 (E.D. Wash. & D. Nev. 1962), aff'd sub nom, United Air Lines, Inc. v. Wiener, 335 F.2d 379 (9th Cir., 1964), cert den, 379 U.S. 951, 88 S. Ct. 452, 13 L. Ed. 2d 548 (1964) (applying Nevada law); NEW HAMPSHIRE: Bricker v. Crane, 118 N.H. 249, 387 A.2d 321, 324 (1978); Sanderson v. Balfour, 109 N.H. 213, 247 A.2d 185, 187 (1968); NEW JERSEY: New Jersey Manufacturers Insurance Co. v. Browner, 161 N.J. Super. 293, 391 A.2d 923, 926 (1978); Continental Can Co. v. Hudson Foam Latex Products, Inc., 129 N.J. Super. 426, 324 A.2d 60 (1974); NEW YORK: B. R. DeWitt, Inc. v. Hall, 19 N.Y. 2d 141, 225 N.E. 2d 195, 278 N.Y.S. 2d 596 (1967); OHIO: Hicks v. De La Cruz, 52 Ohio St. 2d 71, 369 N.E. 2d 776 (1977); OREGON: State Farm Fire & Casualty Co. v. Century Home Components, Inc., 275 Or. 97, 550 P.2d 1185 (1976); PENNSYLVANIA: In Re Estate of Ellis, 460 Pa. 281, 333 A.2d 728 (1975); UTAH: Norman v. Murray First Thrift & Loan Co., 596 P.2d 1028 (Utah 1979); VIRGINIA: Bates v. Devers, 202 S.E. 2d 917, 921n.7 (Va., 1974) (dictum); Graves v. Associated Transportation, Inc., 344 F.2d 894 (4th Cir., 1965) (interpreting Virginia law); WASHINGTON: Dunlap v. Wild, 22 Wash. App. 583, 591 P.2d 834 (1979); Lange v. Heglund, 391 F. Supp. 128, 130 (W.D. Wash., 1974) (interpreting Washington law); and WISCONSIN: McCourt v. Algiers, 4 Wis. 2d 607, 91 N.W. 2d 194 (1956).

Cases that have allowed defensive use of collateral estoppel while specifically prohibiting offensive use include: Russell v. Atlas Van Lines, Inc., 411 F. Supp. 111, 114–115 (E.D. Okla., 1976); Standage Ventures, Inc. v. State, 114 Ariz. 480, 562 P.2d 360, 364 (1977); Goolaby v. Derby, 189 N.W. 2d 909, 916–917 (Iowa 1971); Home Owners Federal Savings & Loan Association v. Northwest Fire & Marine Insurance Co., 354 Mass. 448, 238 N.E. 2d 55, 59 (1968); see also Environmental Defense Fund, Inc. v. Alexander, 501 F. Supp. 742, 750 (N.D. Miss., 1980) (courts more reluctant to allow offensive use than defensive use).

249. 378 F2d 876 (5th Cir., 1967), cert den 389 US 1009 (1967); lower court opinion is 247 F Supp 851 (ED La., 1965).

250. Id. at pp. 878–879. See generally 67 Iowa L Rev 917 (1982).

251. See National Equipment Rental, Ltd. v. Szukhent, 375 US 311 (1964) at pp. 315–316.

252. See Lipp v. National Screen Service Corp., 290 F2d 321 (3rd Cir., 1961), cert den 368 US 835 (1961).

253. See International Shoe Co. v. Washington, 326 US 310 (1945) at p. 316.

254. See Insurance Corporation of Ireland, Ltd. v. Compagnie des Bauxites de Guinee, 102 S Ct 2099 (1982) at p. 2107.
255. 402 US 313 (1971). See generally 63 BU L Rev 383 (1983).
256. Id. at p. 329. It should be observed, however, that this statement has been qualified, for "privies" as well as persons who controlled the prior litigation may be bound by prior adjudication; also, judgments in class actions may bind those represented who were not made parties to the action. See Montana v. United States, 440 US 147 (1979), and Hansberry v. Lee, 311 US 32 (1940).
257. 102 S Ct 1148 (1982) at p. 1154.
258. See National Equipment case, supra note 251.
259. See Montana case, supra note 256.
260. Supra note 254.
261. Supra note 256.
262. Id. at p. 155.
263. See generally 49 Texas L Rev 1 (1970).
264. See generally 63 B U L Rev 383 (1983).
265. Supra note 257.
266. See Grannis v. Ordean, 234 US 385 (1914) at p. 394.
267. 350 F Supp 757 (SD Ohio, 1972), rev su nom Humphreys v. Tann, 487 F2d 666 (6th Cir., 1973), cert den 416 US 956 (1974).
268. Id. at p. 671.
269. See 81 Harv L Rev 365 (1967) at p. 393.
270. See 1976 Trial Law Guide 249; see 67 Iowa L Rev 917 (1982) at p. 930.
271. See 40 Fordham L Rev 41 (1971); transfer is made in accord with 28 USC 1404(a).
272. See Eisen v. Carlisle & Jacquelin, 417 US 156 (1974).
273. See generally 67 Harv L Rev 1059 (1954).
274. See 35 Yale L J 607 (1926).
275. Section 13 and 14 (1982).
276. Sections 43 to 47 of Restatement (Second) of Judgments.
277. Section 46 thereof.
278. Sections 57 and 58 thereof.
279. Section 39 thereof.
280. Section 41 thereof.
281. Section 40 thereof.
282. 658 F2d 1106 (6th Cir., 1981), cert den 445 US 952 (1981).
283. 291 US 431 (1934).
284. 444 US 286 (1980).
285. See generally 66 Corn L Q 510 (1981).
286. 380 US 545 (1965).
287. Id. at p. 552.
288. Supra note 272.
289. Joint Anti-Fascist Committee v. McGrath, 341 US 123 (1951) at pp. 171–172.
290. 389 US 486 (1968).
291. Rule 24 (a) of FRCP sets forth three criteria for intervention as of right: the nature of the would-be intervenor's interest, the effect that disposition of the action will have on that interest, and the adequacy of any representation of the interest by existing parties.

292. See generally 1982 Ariz St L J 45 (1982).
293. See generally 14 Clearing House Rev 19 (1980).
294. 609 F2d 1291 (9th Cir., 1980).
295. Id. at p. 1293.
296. 481 F Supp 616 (ND Cal., 1979).
297. 479 F Supp 392 (ND Cal., 1979).
298. Peterson v. Sheran, 474 F Supp 1215 (D Minn., 1979) at p. 1219.
299. 365 US 167 (1961).
300. See generally 83 Harv L Rev 1672 (1970) and 88 Harv L Rev 373 (1974).
301. See Chaisson v. Southcoast Corp., 350 US 899 (1955).
302. 340 US 36 (1950).
303. Id. at p. 39.
304. See Hirsch v. Pick-Mt. Laurel Corp., 436 F Supp 1342 (D N.J., 1977), for example; and Section 7.1 herein.
305. 561 F2d 671 (7th Cir., 1977), cert den 435 US 942 (1978).
306. 439 US 1070 (1979).
307. 623 F Supp 1189 (ED Tenn., 1985).
308. 15 USC 1334.
309. Supra note 206 at p. 1191.
310. 781 F2d 394 (5th Cir., 1986).
311. 304 US 64 (1938).
312. 451 US 77 (1981).
313. See United States v. Pastos, 781 F2d 747 (9th Cir., 1986).
314. 440 US 147 (1979).
315. Id. at p. 163.
316. See 128 U Penna L Rev 1471 (1980) at pp. 1484 et seq.
317. 466 F Supp 514 (ED Mo., 1978), rev 606 F2d 795 (8th Cir., 1979), cert granted 100 S Ct 1012 (1980).
318. 449 US 90 (1980).
319. Id. at p. 94.
320. Id. at p. 96:

This Court has never directly decided whether the rules of res judicata and collateral estoppel are generally applicable to 1983 actions. But in *Preiser* v. *Rodriguez*, 411 U.S. 475, 497, the Court noted with implicit approval the view of other federal courts that res judicata principles fully apply to civil rights brought under that statute. See also *Huffman* v. *Pursue, Ltd.*, 420 U.S. 592, 606, n. 18; *Wolff* v. *McDonnell*, 418 U.S. 539, 554, n. 12. . . . And the virtually unanimous view of the Courts of Appeals since *Preiser* has been that 1983 presents no categorical bar to the application of res judicata and collateral estoppel concepts. . . . These federal appellate court decisions have spoken with little explanation or citation in assuming the compatibility of 1983 and rules of preclusion, but the statute and its legislative history clearly support the courts' decisions.

321. Id. at p. 103.
322. Id. at pp. 103–104:

For reasons already discussed at length, nothing in the language or legislative history of 1983 proves any congressional intent to deny binding effect to a state-court judgment or decision when the state court, acting within its proper jurisdiction, has given the parties a full and fair opportunity to litigate federal claims, and thereby has shown itself willing and able to protect federal rights. And nothing in the legislative history of 1983 reveals any purpose to afford less deference to judgments in state criminal proceedings than to those in state civil proceedings. . . . There is, in short, no reason to believe that Congress intended to provide a person claiming a federal right an unrestricted opportunity to relitigate an issue already decided in state court simply because the issue arose in a state proceeding in which he would rather not have been engaged at all.

323. See Greater Boston Television Corp. v. FCC, 444 F2d 841 (DC Cir., 1970), cert den 403 US 923 (1971).

324. 421 F2d 92 (9th Cir., 1970).

325. Id. at p. 103.

326. 341 US 41 (1951).

327. NYLJ (Aug 23, 1985) at p. 13.

328. 48 NY2d 15, 421 NYS2d 35 (1979).

329. 9 NY2d 195, 213 NYS2d 39 (1961), modifying 7 AD2d 968, 183 NYS2d 46 (1959), which modified 12 Misc2d 883, 178 NYS2d 407 (1958).

330. William O. Douglas, "Stare Decisis," 49 Columbia L Rev 735 (1949).

331. See Henderson and Pearson, The Torts Process (1981), at pp. 83–85. Also note 4 Ariz L Rev 39 (1962), 40 Yale L J 161 (1930), and 21 Wayne L Rev 1043 (1975).

332. See Radin, Handbook of Anglo-American Legal History (1936), at p. 355. Also see 4 Pace L Rev (1983) at pp. 18 et seq.

333. See 4 Pace L Rev (1983) at p. 19.

334. See Llewellyn, "Impressions of the Conference on Precedent," Jurisprudence: Realism in Theory and Practice (1962), at p. 126.

335. See 27 Cath Lawyer (1982) at p. 327.

336. 309 US 106 (1940).

337. (Cooley's ed., 1884) at pp. 69–70.

338. See generally 59 St. John's L Rev 445 (1985).

339. Cardozo, The Nature of the Judicial Process (1921), at p. 149.

340. 29 NY2d 527, 272 NE2d 574 (1971).

341. 39 NY2d 493, 348 NE2d 905 (1976).

342. Former Section 5-3.3 of the Estates, Powers and Trusts Law, repealed in 1981.

343. 48 AD2d 61, 368 NYS2d 28 (1975), rev 39 NY2d 493, 348 NE2d 905 (1976).

344. Supra note 338 at p. 451.

345. See generally 14 Wayne L Rev 3-17 (1967).

346. See 51 Fordham L Rev (1982) at p. 57.

347. See (1966) 1 W L R 1234, cited in 80 Harv L Rev 797 (1967) at pp. 797–798, and also Judicial Courts Law, Article 33 (Israel, 1957).

348. 383 F2d 709 (4th Cir., 1967).

349. Id. at p. 714.

350. At pp. 150–151.

351. See Codling v. Paglia, 32 NY2d 330, 298 NE2d 622 (1973).

352. 29 NY2d 356, 278 NE2d 619 (1972).

353. Supra note 338 at p. 454.

354. 39 NY2d 479, 348 NE2d 894 (1976).

355. Id.

356. 383 US 413 (1966).

357. 354 US 376 (1957).

358. 102 AD2d 236 (1984).

359. See Edwin Patterson, Essentials of Insurance Law (1935), at p. 418.

360. See generally Vance On Insurance (1951) at pp. 471 et seq.

361. Globe Mutual Life Insurance Co. v. Wolff, 95 US 326 (1877) at p. 333.

362. Commercial Insurance Co. v. Burnquist, 105 F Supp 920 (ND Ia., 1956), as reported in Richards On Insurance (5th ed. by Warren Freedman, 1952 and 1958) at Section 429.

363. 362 F2d 985 (5th Cir., 1966).

364. 177 NW 242 (Mich., 1920).

365. 264 F2d 440 (7th Cir., 1959).

366. 176 NE 446 (Ohio, 1931).

367. City of Pittsburgh v. Firemen's Insurance Co., 76 A2d 368 (Pa., 1950).

368. 98 NW 227 (Wis., 1904).

369. 176 NW2d 314 (Wis., 1970).

370. 79 Pa 475 (1876).

371. 199 NE 337 (Mass., 1936).

372. Id.

373. 236 SW 278 (Ark., 1921).

374. Klingman v. National Indemnity Co., 317 F2d 859 (7th Cir., 1963).

375. 427 F2d 1355 (9th Cir., 1977).

376. 330 F2d 142 (5th Cir., 1964).

377. See Pollock v. Connecticut Fire Insurance Co., 199 NE 816 (Ill., 1935).

378. See Blades v. Farmers & Bankers Life Insurance Co., 235 P 1082 (Kan., 1924).

379. See Arneberg v. Continental Casualty Co., 190 NW 97 (Wis., 1922).

380. Supra note 362: i.e., Section 423 of Richards On Insurance.

381. 96 US 234 (1878).

382. Id.:

> Forfeitures are not favored in the law. They are often the means of great oppression and injustice. And, where adequate compensation can be made, the law in many cases, and equity in all cases, discharges the forfeiture, upon such compensation being made. It is true, we held in Statham's case, 93 U.S. 24 [XXIII, 789], that, in life insurance, time of payment is material, and cannot be extended by the courts against the assent of the Company. But where such assent is given, the courts should be liberal in construing the transaction in favor of avoiding a forfeiture.

383. 165 NW 482 (Minn., 1917).

384. 178 A 859 (R.I., 1935).

385. 123 So2d 598 (Ala., 1960).

386. 148 SE 179 (S.C., 1929).

387. 32 A 439 (Pa., 1895).

388. Id. at p. 440.

389. 493 SW2d 748 (Tex., 1973).

390. Id. at p. 750.

391. 675 P2d 703 (Ariz., 1983).

392. See Nicolletti v. Westcor, Inc., 639 P2d 330 (Ariz., 1982), in which the motion for summary judgment was not opposed by the insured because of an agreement between the insured and Vagnozzi that Vagnozzi would not execute any judgment against the insured if the insured agreed not to contest the motion for summary judgment on the issue of negligence, which fact of negligence would bring the accident within the coverage of the insurance policy.

393. See Globe Indemnity Co. v. Blomfield, 562 P2d 1372 (Ariz., 1977); see generally 27 Ariz L Rev (1985) at pp. 243 et seq.

394. Supra note 391 at p. 707.
395.

(1) When an indemnitor has an obligation to indemnify an indemnitee (such as an insured) against liability to third persons and also to provide the indemnitee with a defense of actions involving claims that might be within the scope of the indemnity obligation, and an action is brought against the indemnitee involving such a claim and the indemnitor is given reasonable notice of the action and an opportunity to assume its defense, a judgment for the insured person has the following effects on the indemnitor in a subsequent action by the indemnitee for indemnification:

(a) The indemnitor is estopped from disputing the existence and extent of the indemnitee's liability to the injured person; and

(b) The indemnitor is precluded from relitigating those issues determined in the action against the indemnitee as to which there was no conflict of interest between the indemnitor and the indemnitee.

(2) A "conflict of interest" for purposes of this Section exists when the injured person's claim against the indemnitee is such that it could be sustained on different grounds, one of which is within the indemnitor's obligation to indemnify and another of which is not.

396. See 27 Ariz L Rev (1985) at p. 254.
397. Id. at p. 252.
398. See Chapter 5 herein.
399. 410 F2d 718 (5th Cir., 1969); also note 31 ALR3d 1044.
400. 238 NE2d 55 (Mass., 1968).
401. 614 F2d 160 (8th Cir., 1980).
402. See 14 Creighton L Rev 1181 (1981).
403. See, for example, Maryland Casualty Co. v. Fidelity & Casualty Co. of New York, 313 F Supp 500 (WD Mo., 1970); Lemar Towing Co., Inc. v. Fireman's Fund Insurance Co., 352 F Supp 652 (ED La., 1972), cert den 414 US 976 (1973); and Prime Drilling Co. v. Standard Accident Insurance Co., 287 F2d 316 (7th Cir., 1961), cert den 386 US 826 (1961).
404. ——NYS2d——(July 10, 1986).
405. 616 F2d 111 (5th Cir., 1980).
406. Id. at p. 116.
407. 406 F Supp 484 (D Ohio, 1985).
408. 352 NE2d 817 (Ind App., 1985).
409. 516 F Supp 31 (SD Ga., 1981).
410. 480 F Supp 600 (ED Va., 1979).
411. 443 NE2d 978 (Ohio, 1985).
412. See generally 15 New Eng L Rev 1 (1979).
413. See footnote 116 at p. 23 thereof.
414. 315 F2d 449 (1st Cir., 1963), cert den 375 US 820 (1963).
415. 488 F Supp 836 (ED Tex., 1980).
416. Id. at pp. 841–842.
417. 663 SW2d 816 (Tex., 1984).
418.

In the case at bar, it is not prior litigation or the doctrine of collateral estoppel that determines the Bonniwells' rights. Those rights are determined by the settlement contract voluntarily made by the Bonniwells for valuable consideration. Their decision to enter this agreement was in no way influenced by Beech. That decision cannot justly be given the effect of denying to Beech the benefits of its successful litigation of its rights against Metro and Shawnee. Nor should that agreement of the parties be permitted to obstruct the operation of the legal doctrine of collateral estoppel. [p. 823]

419. Barson v. E. R. Squibb Corp., 682 P2d 832 (Utah, 1984).
420. Vacarro v. E. R. Squibb Corp.,——NYS2d——(1985).
421. Citing Vincent v. Thompson, 50 AD2d 211 (1975) at p. 221.
422. 564 SW2d 195 (Tex Civ App., 1978).
423. 629 F Supp 1160 (SD Tex., 1986).
424. Decided June 24, 1986.
425. Id.

Initially, we note that the omission of the statute of limitations defense in the appellant's amended answer does not constitute a waiver in view of the procedural history of this case, nor would an adjudication of this partial summary judgment motion based upon this unpleaded defense result in surprise to the plaintiff. Under the unusual circumstances of this case and in the absence of prejudice to the plaintiff, who never raised the issue of waiver, postponement of an adjudication of the appellant's motion would serve no purpose (see Rogoff v. San Juan Racing Assn., 77 AD2d 831; cf. Furlo v. Cheek, 20 AD2d 939, 940).

We further note that [a] denial of a motion for summary judgment is not necessarily res judicata or the law of the case that there is an issue of fact in that case that will be established at the trial (Zook v. Hartford Acc. & Ind. Co., 64 AD2d 701, 702).

426. See generally 56 St John's L Rev 171 (1981).
427. 442 NYS2d 554 (1981), aff'g 428 NYS2d 402 (1980).
428. See Gwynn v. Wilhelm, 360 P2d 312 (Ore., 1961), and Leslie v. Mollica, 211 NW 267 (Mich., 1926).
429. See Chapter 5 herein.
430. Id.
431. See 52 Miss L J (1982) at pp. 787 et seq.
432. 346 F2d 532 (2nd Cir., 1965).
433. 439 US 322 (1949).
434. See Humphreys v. Tann, 487 F2d 666 (6th Cir., 1973), cert den 416 US 956 (1974); Price v. Atchison Topeka & Santa Fe Railway Co., 330 P2d 933 (Cal App., 1958); and Montgomery v. Taylor-Green Gas Co., 206 SW2d 919 (Ky., 1947).
435. "Proposed Rules of Civil Procedure," 39 FRD 69 (1966) at p. 103.
436. See McQuillen v. A & R Development Corp., 576 F Supp 1023 (ED Pa., 1983).
437. Id. Also see "Mass Tort Class Actions: Going, Going, Gone?," 98 FRD 323 (1983):

One important, but both under-utilized and overlooked, aspect of Rule 23's repertoire provides the possibility of class adjudication not as an entire case, but limited to one or more issues common to a group of cases. Rule 23(c) (4) (A) provides: When appropriate, an action may be maintained as a class action with respect to particular issues . . . and the provisions of this rule shall then be construed and applied accordingly. Therefore, even when the injuries alleged, or defenses to numerous plaintiffs' claims are different, the court may still maintain a class action to adjudicate any common factual or legal issues. In those cases where many litigants seek recovery for one alleged misconduct of a defendant, *e.g.*, manufacture of a defective product, the court may certify a class action under subdivision (b) (1) or (b) (3), as to the common issues, regardless of how few in number, if the court feels that representative litigation will fairly and economically resolve those common issues. *Id.* at 326–327 (footnote omitted).

438. See Murphy v. Landsburg, 490 F2d 319 (3rd Cir., 1973), cert den 416 US 939 (1974).

439. 717 F2d 767 (3rd Cir., 1983).

440. See Sullivan v. Chase Investment Service of Boston, Inc., 79 FRD 246 (ND Cal., 1978) at p. 265.

441. See Goldstein v. Regal Crest, Inc., 59 FRD 396 (ED Pa., 1973) at p. 400.

442. 104 S Ct 2794 (1984).

443. Supra note 54.

444. 390 US 102 (1967).

445. See 4 Am J Trial Adv 75 (1980), and also note 68 Columbia L Rev 1457 (1969).

446. 384 US 294 (1966).

447. 603 F2d 590 (7th Cir., 1979).

448. 633 F2d 803 (9th Cir., 1980).

449. 627 F2d 996 (9th Cir., 1980).

450. 316 US 149 (1942).

451. 310 US 381 (1940).

452. 463 F Supp 732 (EDNY, 1979).

453. 404 F2d 1059 (5th Cir., 1968), cert den 395 US 920 (1969).

454. Id.:

> Though the issue decided by the Commissioner was the same as the one determined by the jury, there are . . . differences between the two proceedings precluding collateral estoppel. The proceedings before the Commissioner are more "free-wheeling," not only in the quantum of proof necessary to establish a claim, but also in the nature of evidence and procedural rules that are followed. It is well settled that the Commissioner is not bound by the common-law rules of evidence or technical rules of procedure. This laxity is seen in the rule that the admissibility of evidence depends only on whether it is such evidence as a reasonable mind might accept as probative. Thus hearsay evidence is generally admissible if considered reliable. The paramount difference, however, is that in considering the proof offered by the parties the Commissioner operates under the statutory policy that all doubtful fact questions are to be resolved in favor of the injured employee or his dependent family. This policy effectuates the intent of the statute to place "the burden of possible error" on those best able to bear it. Since a jury would not be directed to find for the injured party, as a matter of policy, when the evidence created doubt about the injury, we are convinced that there is a substantial variance in the standard of proof required to establish facts before the Commissioner and the jury. The standard before the jury is the preponderance-of-credible-evidence test. Although we cannot ascribe a legal label to the burden before the Commissioner, the statutory policy, as interpreted by the courts, indicates that it is a less stringent standard of persuasion. . . . Therefore, since we are persuaded that the applicable legal rules enable a claimant to establish the existence of an actionable injury before the Commissioner more easily than in a civil tort action, we agree with the district court that on the facts of this case the doctrine of collateral estoppel is inapplicable.

455. (3rd ed., 1972), Section 18.02.

456. 63 NE2d 68 (N.Y., 1945).

457. 409 F Supp 837 (DC Cir., 1976).

458. 570 F2d 1311 (7th Cir., 1978).

459. Id. at p. 1322.

460. NYS2d (1986).

461. See Section 5 herein.

462. 332 US 380 (1947).
463. Id.:

The oft-quoted observation in Rock Island, Arkansas & Louisiana Railroad Co. v. United States, 254 U.S. 141, 143, that ''Men must turn square corners when they deal with the Government,'' does not reflect a callous outlook. It merely expresses the duty of all courts to observe the conditions defined by Congress for charging the public treasury. The ''terms and conditions'' defined by the Corporation, under authority of Congress, for creating liability on the part of the Government preclude recovery for the loss of the reseeded wheat no matter with what good reason the respondents thought they had obtained insurance from the Government.

464. 104 S Ct 2218 (1984).
465. 698 F2d 615 (3rd Cir., 1983).
466. Supra note 464 at p. 2224.
467. 450 US 785 (1981).
468. See, for example, Sims v. Heckler, 725 F2d 1143 (7th Cir., 1984).
469. 719 F2d 333 (10th Cir., 1983), cert den 104 S Ct 1710 (1984).
470. 518 F Supp 921 (SDNY, 1981).
471. 409 US 232 (1972) at p. 235.
472. 257 F Supp 298 (Md., 1967).
473. See United States v. United Air Lines, Inc., 216 F Supp 709 (D Nev., 1962), aff 335 F2d 379 (9th Cir., 1963), cert den 379 US 951 (1964).
474. 181 F2d 419 (3rd Cir., 1950), cert den 340 US 865 (1951).

On the other hand, the New York Appellate Division, First Dept., in Scruggs-Leftwich v. Rivercross Tenants' Corp. 119 AD2d 88, 505 NYS2d 406, decided July 31, 1986, readily estopped the New York state government whose Division of Housing and Community Renewal (DHCR) had accorded a cooperative apartment building certain privileges with respect to purchasers of shares in the cooperative. According to the court:

DHCR should be estopped from changing the resale procedures currently in effect at Rivercross without a showing of compelling necessity and due consideration to the hardship such changes would cause those stockholders who, in reliance upon the present procedures, made substantial improvements to their apartments or, on resale, purchased such improvements at a significant cost. Special Term refused to apply the doctrine of Estoppel because it found DHCR was acting in a governmental capacity. A governmental agency may be estopped, however, even when acting in its governmental capacity, if a manifest injustice would otherwise occur.

The New York appellate court opined:

Concededly, Estoppel should be invoked ''only in truly exceptional cases, involving as it often does, an intrusion, pro tanto, by the judiciary, into the prerogatives of other branches of the government.'' . . . In our view, enforcement of the Commissioner's order and the indiscriminate ban on the sale of any improvements would result in manifest injustice to those Rivercross stockholders who relied to their financial detriment on the representations . . . and on the conduct and representations of DHCR, with respect to their resale rights.

475. 506 NYS2d 77 (1986).
476. See Clemens v. Apple, 65 NY2d 746 (1980). Arbitration has been defined as ''a proceeding whereby, pursuant to the agreement of the parties, disputes or controversies between them, without regard to the justiciable nature thereof, are submitted by them for determination by an individual or individuals rather than by a court or judge

acting in a judicial capacity.'' Eager, The Arbitration Contract and Proceedings (1971), Section 1.

477. 475 F2d 151 (2nd Cir., 1975).

478. 478 F Supp 766 (SDNY, 1979).

479. Id. at p. 769.

480. See Schultz v. Boy Scouts of America, 65 NY2d 189 (1981).

481. 113 AD2d 941 (1980).

482. 116 AD2d 614, 497 NYS2d 702 (2nd Dept., Jan. 24, 1986).

483. See generally 33 Amer U L Rev 643 (1984).

484. 708 F2d 243 (6th Cir., 1983).

485. See United States v. Hans, 548 F Supp 1119 (SD Ohio, 1982), vacated 684 F2d 343 (6th Cir., 1982).

486. 424 F2d 639 (2nd Cir., 1970), cert den 400 US 827 (1970).

487. See Moore v. United States, 360 F2d 353 (4th Cir., 1965), cert den 385 US 1001 (1967).

488. See Commissioner of Internal Revenue v. Sunnen, 333 US 591 (1947).

489. 43 TC 50 (1964), aff 360 F2d 358 (4th Cir., 1965).

490. See, for example, Overseas Motors, Inc. v. Import Motors, Ltd., 375 F Supp 499 (ED Mich., 1974).

491. 43 TC 68 (1964).

492. See Kercheval v. United States, 274 US 220 (1927), and Plunkett v. Commissioner, 465 F2d 299 (7th Cir., 1972).

493. See Emich Motors Corp. v. General Motors Corp., 340 US 558 (1961) at p. 568; also 13 Wake Forest L Rev 445 (1977).

494. See United States v. Keller, 624 F2d 1154 (3rd Cir., 1980) at p. 1157.

495. 219 Cal Rptr 272 (Cal Ct App., 1985).

496. 695 F2d 521 (11th Cir., 1983).

497. 11 USC 727 (a)(4)(a).

498. See 7 Amer J Trial Adv (1985) at p. 406.

499. 50 NY2d 333, 406 NE2d 783 (1980).

500.

> Although it is true that in civil litigation there has always been greater flexibility as to the identity of the party who seeks to utilize the estoppel than is deemed proper with respect to the identity of the party against whom the estoppel is to be employed, there exist sound policy grounds for not adopting similar rules in a criminal prosecution. For one thing, in the criminal law, in contrast to civil litigation, society has an overwhelming interest in ensuring not merely that the determination of guilt or innocence be made, but that it be made correctly. While the correct resolution of civil disputes is indeed an important goal of our legal system, it may fairly be said that society's primary interest in the resolution of civil disputes is that they be settled in a peaceful, orderly, and impartial manner. Since this is so, it is appropriate that litigation-limiting devices such as the doctrine of collateral estoppel be liberally applied in civil litigation. In contradistinction, it is the correctness of the result which is of preeminent concern in a criminal prosecution, for the major function of a criminal proceeding is the conviction of the guilty and the acquittal of the innocent, not the swift resolution of some private dispute between the prosecutor and the accused. Hence, the civil doctrine of collateral estoppel, which accepts the occasional enthronement of erroneous findings of fact as a necessary cost of conserving the time and resources of the parties and the courts, is of less relevance in the criminal law. [Pp. 345 and 789–790]

501. 163 NW2d 289 (Minn., 1974).

502. 447 US 10 (1980).

503. Id. at pp. 22–24.
504. 463 F Supp 596 (SD Cal., 1978).
505. 649 F2d 1236 (7th Cir., 1981).
506. See generally 11 Williamette L J 176 (1975).
507. 206 A2d 624 (Pa., 1965), cert den 381 US 925 (1965).
508. Id. at p. 626.
509. 466 F Supp 167 (SDNY, 1979).
510. See Marcus v. Sprayregen, 458 F Supp 1216 (SDNY, 1979).
511. 378 F Supp 862 (D DC, 1974).
512. 494 F2d 145 (2nd Cir., 1974), cert den 419 US 828 (1974).
513. 424 F Supp 1108 (WD Okla., 1976).
514. Id. at p. 1113.
515. See Charles v. Wade, 665 F2d 661 (5th Cir., 1982), cert den 103 S Ct 1426 (1983). See generally 131 U Penna L Rev 1209 (1983).
516. See generally 19 Ariz L Rev 349 (1977).
517. See United States v. Throckmorton, 98 US 61 (1878) at p. 65.
518. 3 Johns (NY) 157 (1808).
519. Still another aspect of criminal conduct was discussed in Parsons Steel Co. v. First Alabama Bank, decided in July 1986 by the U.S. Supreme Court 106 S Ct 768. Here an Alabama husband and wife who owned a steel company charged that the defendant bank had criminally defrauded them; they sued the bank in civil actions in both the state and federal courts, and lost in the federal court but won in the Alabama state court. The bank appealed to the Eleventh U.S. Court of Appeals, arguing that the state court had wrongly decided that the federal court verdict did not preclude the plaintiffs from proceeding with the state court suit. The federal appellate court agreed with the bank and enjoined the state court from entering the verdict; but the U.S. Supreme Court in an opinion by Justice William Rehnquist reversed, holding that a federal district court or a federal appellate court cannot enjoin a state proceeding even after finding that the state court had incorrectly interpreted the effect of a prior federal ruling.
520. See, for example, The Queen v. Miles, 24 Qbd 423 (1890) at p. 431.
521. 225 US 436 (1912) at p. 444.
522. See Potomac Dredging Co. v. Smoot, 69 A 507 (Md., 1908).
523. See Skelly Oil Co. v. Butner, 205 P2d 15 (Okla., 1949).
524. 197 NYS 2d 1001 (1959).
525. See Logan v. Union Sulpher Co., 29 F Supp 33 (D La., 1939).
526. 112 SE2d 81 (N.C., 1960).
527. See Ramsey v. Kitchen, 15 SE2d 877 (Ga., 1941).
528. See Greenleaf on Evidence (1866) at Section 279 thereof.
529. See Kunihiro v. Lyons Bros. Co., 12 F2d 894 (9th Cir., 1926), cert den 47 S Ct 1121 (1926).
530. Section 1230 of Tiffany on Real Property (Jones ed., 1939):

> It has been frequently said that an estoppel by deed binds not only parties but also privies, and a like statement is ordinarily made in regard to estoppel by misrepresentation. Strictly applying such a rule, the estoppel would operate against a subsequent grantee although he is a purchaser for value without notice of the prior conveyance by his grantor. And there are a considerable number of cases which appear to adopt such a view, that the subsequent grantee is estopped to assert the after-acquired title of his grantor, as against a prior grantee of the latter, without reference to whether such subsequent grantee has or has not notice of the prior conveyance. In some cases, however, a contrary view is asserted, expressly or by implication, that the subsequent grantee is

not bound by the estoppel unless he had notice of the prior conveyance by his grantor. In several of these latter cases the question chiefly discussed is whether the subsequent grantee is charged with notice by the record of the prior conveyance, this occurring before his grantor acquired title. This question has ordinarily been answered in the negative, that is, the purchaser was regarded as under no obligation to search the records under his grantor in order to discover any conveyance made by the latter after acquiring title. A contrary view would impose on every purchaser the very serious burden of searching the records for conveyances made not only by his vendor, but also by his vendor's predecessors in title, for an indefinite time back of the date of his or their acquisition of title. [Section 1234]

531. See generally 50 ALR 666.

532. See 76 ALR 297, and note Williston on Contracts, Section 739; also Williams v. Reid, 37 SW2d 537 (Mo., 1933).

533. 81 P2d 944 (Cal., 1938).

534. 6 P2d 317 (Cal., 1931).

535. See Provident Security Life Insurance Co. v. Gorsuch, 323 F2d 839 (9th Cir., 1963), cert den 376 US 950 (1964).

536. See generally 31 Tenn L Rev 336 (1964).

537. See Kingsley v. English, 278 NW 154 (Minn., 1938), and 115 ALR 654 (1938).

538. See J & J Builders Supply Co. v. Caffin, 248 Cal App2d 299 (1967). Also note Section 16 of the Uniform Partnership Act.

539. See Hobbs v. Triangle Supply Co., 378 SW2d 726 (Tex. Civ App., 1964).

540. For example, see Section 13.1-119 of Virginia Stock Corporation Act (1957).

541. See Nelson v. Coney, 80 So2d 476 (Miss., 1955).

542. See Hoffman v. Hoffman, 161 NE 723 (Ill., 1928).

543. See Rhoads v. Rhoads, 119 SW2d 247 (Mo., 1938).

544. Armijo v. Town of Atrisco, 239 P2d 535 (N.M., 1951).

545. See Woods v. Cannaday, 158 F2d 184 (DC Cir., 1946).

546. See Pine v. M. E. Conran Co., 51 NYS2d 34 (1944).

547. ——F2d——(2nd Cir., 1986).

548. 279 A2d 450 (R.I., 1971).

549. See generally 65 Harv L Rev 818 (1952). Note United States v. Moser, 266 US 236 (1924), where the highest court opined:

> [A] fact, question or right distinctly adjudged in the original action cannot be disputed in a subsequent action, even though the determination was reached upon an erroneous view or by an erroneous application of the law. That would be to affirm the principle in respect of the thing adjudged but, at the same time, deny it all efficacy by sustaining a challenge to the grounds upon which the judgment was based. [Citations omitted.] A determination in respect of the status of an individual upon which his right to recover depends is as conclusive as a decision upon any other matter. [p. 242]

550. 37 Pa Super 496.

551. See 140 ALR 901, and also see Lippincott v. Lippincott, 3 NW2d 207 (Neb., 1942).

552. See Carpenter v. Thompson, 3 NH 204 (1868).

553. See generally 38 Columbia L Rev 292 (1938).

554. 298 P2d 598 (Cal App, 1956).

555. See generally 73 Harv L Rev 1410 (1960).

556. See Section 47 (b) of Restatement (Second) of Judgments.

557. See generally 39 Iowa L Rev 255 (1954).

558. Section 68, Comment (a) of Restatement (Second) of Judgments.

559. Note Moore v. Harjo, 144 F2d 318 (10th Cir., 1944), for example.

560. See Middlesex Concrete Products & Excavating Corp. v. Borough of Carteret, 113 A2d 821 (N.J., 1955).

561. See also London v. City of Philadelphia, 194 A2d 901 (Pa., 1963); cf. Phoenix Insurance Co. v. Haney, 108 So2d 227 (Miss., 1959).

562. 343 P2d 977 (Cal App., 1959).

563. 30 FRD 540 (MD Tenn., 1962).

564. 341 NYS2d 767 (1973).

565. See 6 Wright & Miller, Federal Practice and Procedure, Section 1410 (1971).

566. See Libbey-Owens-Ford Glass Co. v. Sylvania Industrial Corp., 154 F2d 814 (2nd Cir., 1946), cert den 328 US 859 (1946).

567. See In Matter of Farrell Publishing Corp., 130 F Supp 449 (SDNY, 1955).

568. See Koufakis v. Carvel, 425 F2d 892 (2nd Cir., 1970).

569. Supra note 565.

570. 317 SE2d 408 (N.C., 1984).

571. 200 NE 2nd 345 (Ohio App., 1964).

572. Note that the affidavit of the insurance company made it appear

1. that defendant does not deny liability upon the policy in question;
2. that there are two claimants for the face value of the policy to the exclusion of each other;
3. that both claimants are residents of California, including the plaintiff herein;
4. that service upon both was had in California;
5. that the other claimant as a resident of California is not subject to the jurisdiction of the courts of Ohio;
6. documentary proof of presentation of claim and demand for payment by the other claimant, mother of this plaintiff, and proof of basis upon which mother's claim is founded;
7. that defendant is willing to pay the proceeds of the policy to the lawful beneficiary but that it does not know which beneficiary has the better claim at law;
8. that in the interpleader action the California court has jurisdiction of the subject matter as well as both claimants and has the power to decree complete and final justice to all persons interested in the subject matter.

573. See Wolfe Investments, Inc. v. Shroyer, 402 P2d 516 (Ore., 1965).

574. See Aldrich v. Transcontinental Land and Water Co., 281 P2d 362 (Cal App., 1955).

575. See Section 10.6 herein.

576. See Daly v. White, 222 P2d 950 (Cal App., 1950).

577. See Lord v. Garland, 168 P2d 5 (Cal App., 1946).

578. See generally 38 Yale L J 299 (1929). Also see generally 65 Harv L Rev 818 (1952).

579. 333 US 591 (1948).

580. See Sisemore v. Neal, 367 SW2d 417 (Ark., 1963).

581. See Standard Accident Insurance Co. v. Doiron, 170 F2d 206 (1st Cir., 1948).

582. Note Section 93 (1) of Restatement (Second) of Judgments.

583. Id., Section 93 (2).

584. Section 105 of Restatement (Second) of Judgments.
585. Id., Section 103.
586. See, for example, Dulak v. Dulak, 496 SW2d 776 (Tex Civ App., 1973).
587. Supra note 584 at Section 87.
588. See 1B Moore, Federal Practice, Section 0.411 (10).
589. 249 P2d 264 (Cal., 1952).
590. Id.:

The rule respecting such judgments is illustrative of the line that has been drawn beyond which a plaintiff may not go if he hopes thereafter to start again. It is analogous to the rule that was applicable to nonsuits before section 581c was added to the Code of Civil Procedure in 1947. A judgment of nonsuit was not on the merits, and a plaintiff could start anew and recover judgment if he could prove sufficient facts in the second action.

591. 7 NY2d 287, 165 NE2d 156 (1959).

Bibliography

20 Tulsa Law Journal 1 (1984).

1985 Annual Survey of American Law (NYU) 206 (1985).

Case & Comment (Jan.–Feb. 1987) 22.

Trial Magazine (Dec. 1986) 80.

Tort & Insurance Law Journal (1987) 71.

National Law Journal (Dec. 1, 1986) 22.

21 Israel Law Review 165 (1986).

Symposium: Preclusion, 70 Ia. L. Rev. No. 1 (1984).

Ruth Bader Ginsburg, "The Work of Professor Allan Delker Vestal," 13.

David L. Shapiro, "Should a Guilty Plea Have Preclusive Effect?," 27.

Robert C. Casad, "Issue Preclusion and Foreign Country Judgments: Whose Law?," 53.

Geoffrey C. Hazard, Jr., "Preclusion as to Issues of Law: The Legal System's Interest," 81.

Lea Brilmayer, "Credit Due Judgments and Credit Due Laws: The Respective Roles of Due Process and Full Faith and Credit in the Interstate Context," 95.

A. Leo Levin and Susan M. Leeson, "Issue Preclusion Against the United States Government," 113.

Michael D. Green, "The Inability of Offensive Collateral Estoppel to Fulfill Its Promise: An Examination of Estoppel in Asbestos Litigation," 141.

T. L. Mann. "Restrictions upon the Use of Nonmutual Collateral Estoppel Where the Government Is a Party. (United States v. Mendoza, 104 S. Ct. 568 (1984)." 24 Washburn Law Journal 121 (1984).

"A Prior Guilty Plea Is Sufficient to Raise and Establish the Affirmative Defense of Collateral Estoppel. Prinz v. Greate Bay Casino Corp. (1983)." 29 Villanova Law Review 857 (1984).

Symposium: Preclusion in a Federal System, 70 Cornell L. Rev. (1985).

Robert C. Casad, ''Introduction,'' 509.

Judith Resnik, ''Precluding Appeals,'' 603.

Stephen B. Burbank, ''Interjurisdictional Preclusion and Federal Common Law: Toward a General Approach,'' 625.

Geoffrey C. Hazard, Jr., ''Reflections on the Substance of Finality,'' 642.

Judith Resnik, ''Further Reflections,'' 653.

Stephen B. Burbank, ''Afterwords: A Response to Professor Hazard and a Comment on Marrese,'' 659.

''*Res Judicata* Effects of Involuntary Dismissals,'' 667.

''*Res Judicata* Effects of State Agency Decisions in Title VII Actions,'' 695.

''*Res Judicata* Effects of Unappealed, Independently Sufficient Alternative Determinations,'' 717.

Index to Cases

Subject Index

About the Author

WARREN FREEDMAN, member of the New York, Federal, and U.S. Supreme Court bars, served as corporate counsel to Bristol-Myers Company for 20 years in addition to his private law practice. He is the author of *The Right of Privacy in the Computer Age, Frivolous Lawsuits and Frivolous Defenses, Federal Statutes on Environmental Protection, Professional Sports and Antitrust* (all Quorum Books, 1987), *Foreign Plaintiffs in Products Liability Actions* (Quorum Books, 1988), *Hazardous Waste Liability, International Products Liability Law* (3 vols.), *Products Liability for Corporate Counsels, Controllers, and Products Safety Executives, Allergy and Products Liability,* and *Richards on Insurance,* as well as two travel books and three sociology textbooks. Over the years he has contributed extensively to various law journals and reviews. He has taught on the graduate level at Rutgers University School of Law and the New School for Social Research.